BREAKING
BUBBLES

—————————— AND ——————————

GARY KENDALL

Cover Art and Illustrations by
Ingrid Maria Ericsson

To Ulla

Table of Contents

List of Meditations and Healing Practices

Preface

I want to invite you to the joy and the freedom that *breaking bubbles* can bring into your life. At the heart of this book are stories of the healings of people who have found a way to break through the persistent obstacles in their lives and to step into a different relationship with their identity and their spiritual life. And I want to say right from the start that I hope that you too will find valuable openings for your personal growth and spiritual development here—new insights into how you can release the limitations in your life—by *breaking bubbles*. In particular, this book attempts to inspire the kind of insights and experiences that might lift your level of consciousness—maybe in ways that take you to a place of greater security and optimism in your spiritual evolution.

This isn't exactly the book I started off to write. In fact, I put away another book draft before the real work on this book truly began. And even then, this book started off in a different direction. It wasn't supposed to be about breaking bubbles, even though pretty clearly a lot of people need to break out of a lot of bubbles. This idea of talking about bubbles entered my spiritual vocabulary pretty slowly. Of course, I heard this metaphor about people being within bubbles used over and over in the media during the time I was writing this book. At the same time, there was no mention of people breaking out of their bubbles. This talk was all about being hopelessly trapped, and the metaphor's usefulness for spiritual work ended right there. At first, I didn't really think very much about any of this. It seemed all so self-evident, and so stuck in rigidity. No, my original goal when I sat down to write this book was to connect the healing of the light-body with collective consciousness. That question had come up in my healing work, and it was my intended focus. Then in the course of pursuing that question, a lot of other information came in.

For three years my wife Ulla and I had made repeated spiritual pilgrimages to northwest Argentina, after which I had published my first book, *We Are The Future Earth: Reflections of a healer's pilgrimage to Argentina's spiritual heartland.* Most of the material for that book had come to me while sitting in the wilderness areas around Cafayate, Argentina, a place that was beneficial for me and amazingly free of human psychic influence, despite its proximity to a great wine-producing area. It was while sitting there for hours in the arid land that the material for that first book had come to me.

It was then in our fourth year after returning again to the same region of Argentina that I began the book that I left behind. I thought that I was going to continue from where the first book had left off. This next book would extend the topics in the first book and go deeper into our relationship with the Earth. To me, that first book was primarily about humanity's relationship with the Earth, and it was secondarily about healing, not healing techniques as much as about the experience of healing and being a healer. My goal was in some large part to inspire others to explore the path of healing, especially in relationship to the Earth.

During that fourth year in Argentina, I wrote numerous chapters for this subsequent book, and the horizon of my spiritual world continued to expand. In particularly it expanded in my relationship to the 'highly evolved worlds,' what I came to call a confederation of beings who had long since passed their ascension and had joined together across the vast spaces of the Cosmos. They seemed to have nothing in common in terms of their origins, but they had all evolved to a very high level of consciousness. You might say that they had completed all but the final steps in their spiritual evolution, and they now stood in a special place to assist others. But they had no interest in intervening in anyone's evolution, and they seemed most dedicated to honoring the diversity of all beings who are evolving toward Oneness in their own way. One of these worlds, the closest one to the Earth, is Antares. In a previous visit to Argentina Ulla and I had experienced a strong awakening with Goddess Antares that is described in my first book. We were profoundly affected by the purity and clarity of the special consciousness of Antares, and we continued striving to understand it as we continued our work in Argentina. That connection to Antares for me evolved into my connection with the highly evolved worlds, while for Ulla her work with Antares grew deeper and led to her Swedish book *Profetia: Möten med Gudinnan Antares och vägen in i femte dimensionen* (in English: *Prophecy: Meeting with the Goddess Antares and the way into the fifth dimension*).

At the end of our fourth year in Argentina, on the very day we were about to return home and on our way to the taxi that would take us to the international airport, Ulla tripped on the sidewalk and bumped her knee. She got up and hobbled to the taxi, but by the time we arrived at the airport she couldn't walk. Only when we finally arrived home in Sweden did we discover that she had broken her kneecap. The whole next year was focused on her recovery with our energy devoted to getting her knee ready for another trip to Argentina. It was not our best year, but one year after Ulla's accident, she was indeed ready to walk out again into the arid lands around Cafayate.

Maybe Ulla's fall was just an accident in the ordinary sense, but that last year also led me to a total dead end in my writing.

I believed that what I had written during that last trip had some significant parts, and maybe I will finish that book one day, but it was somehow at odds with what ultimately needed to come through me. I felt like I had to search to find some new foundation for myself and for my writing. During all of this time, I had, of course, continued to work with clients and to gather ideas about healing that I might share. So, there was an evolution that was taking place in my healing work, even if it felt like my writing had hit a roadblock.

It was right before Ulla and I returned to Argentina for the fifth time, that I experienced a healing session that I describe in Part 3 in which I caught a glimpse of how collective consciousness was influencing people's individual healing. So, when returning to Argentina the following year, I asked specifically for guidance about healing and the collective. I needed some new fundamental understanding.

And then the material poured in! I didn't have any feeling of inventing that material. I received it. I simply asked questions and then a voice spoke to me about things that I had never understood before. And none of this information was about me personally. I wasn't asking questions about myself. It was about the collective and the individual, about the nature of consciousness—and bubbles. And I particularly wanted to understand the impact of collective consciousness on healing. I was like a reporter—asking questions and recording the answers. It seemed that everyday some new aspect of the topic would be revealed to me, and my notes were filled with the most amazing discussions. These were topics about which a huge amount of information was ready to be revealed. Each day Ulla and I would head off into some place in the wilderness along with our companions Kerstin Brodin and Lis Gerhardt. Each day we would gather in the late afternoon before supper and share our day's experiences. There were interesting stories developing for each one of us.

You might want to ask about the exact source of this material. I choose not to channel messages in the usual sense. The commentaries I received were directed to me, and many of my sessions seemed like dialogs in which my search for answers led me deeper and deeper into unknown territory. Who was answering? I would say it was a very open aspect of myself, one that was in relationship with the highly evolved worlds. The voice spoke, and I recorded the answers. I do not literally quote any of this material here in the book, although the original questions and answers sometimes make for interesting reading, but the order and progression of the ideas as they came forth probably jumped around too much for an outside reader. So I have rewritten everything and reorganized it into a form appropriate for presentation in a book.

And while much of the book's material arose in Argentina, the constant backdrop of the book is my healing work back in Stockholm. Healing as a path for spiritual growth is a core topic. During the months between our trips to Argentina, Ulla and I had been busy doing healings, holding workshops, and constantly discussing our work. The workshops were often the test-bed for new ideas about healing, and our approaches had evolved a great deal over these years. For example, the central importance of people being the creators of their own lives and therefore the creator of their own limitations—that emerged in response to our healing work. And, of course, I make reference in this book to numerous clients I have seen over the years. I have been careful to obscure the true identities of all these clients. In truth, the people described here are all composites of many clients I have seen. For example, Ella is a composite of several clients who to me had similar issues. I think that all of my examples are inspired by the healings of actual people even if the details of their lives have been altered.

And I must express my gratitude to all of these clients for everything that they have taught me about the nature of healing and personal growth.

As I sat down in Stockholm to begin work on this book, I struggled with issues of organization. It seemed that all of the subtopics were so tightly interwoven. For example, Oneness was a thread through everything. The consciousness of Antares and my connection to the highly evolved worlds brought me new insights, but I struggled with how to convey these insights and still maintain the high frequency of the original language that had been given to me in Argentina. I ultimately realized that the book had to start from the very beginning with the most fundamental concept: Oneness.

I was many months into the writing of this book when I asked Ulla for advice on the title. My original title would have been "Healing As A Creator Being," but no one liked that title. Ulla had read through numerous draft chapters, and pointed out something that I had missed: the concept of bubbles was explicitly part of the material on collective consciousness—but it was essentially implied everywhere else in the book. Clearly, 'bubbles' was a unifying thread, even if I hadn't started off writing the text that way. After a change of title, the material and the organization began to fall into place. I realized from the start that the concept of 'bubbles' might strike readers as whimsical or provocative—so be it—whereas I came to understand 'bubbles' as, in fact, a truly fundamental phenomenon. It is a bit like discovering the forest in the midst of the trees. We are so focused on our individual issues that we miss the obvious universality of 'bubbles' and the way that their boundaries hold us in a limited reality. The limiting effect of being within our bubbles hides their very existence from us. I thought that the topic needed to be grounded in the practical experience of healing in order to be made relevant to everyday life and also reveal its true depth. For that reason, I introduce 'bubbles' one step at a time. And I must give thanks to the other people who have helped me to bring forth this book, especially Peter Edler who contributed the primary editing. And there were many important suggestions from Katarina Chowra, Lis Gerhardt, Eva Wiger, and Anne Wells.

Some other points about the goals of the book and my background may be helpful to the reader:

- Amorah Quan Yin who founded the Dolphin Star Temple Mystery School was my primary teacher. My main inspiration for the 'path of healing' was Amorah. Her teachings often described as Pleiadian Lightwork are a foundation for this book. Try visiting http://www.dolphinstartemple.org/.
- I also studied for many years with shamanic healers from Peru who helped me to find my relationship with the Earth and to expand my heartfulness. They are the other major spiritual inspiration in my life.
- For all of my adult life I have been a teacher of music, and music is always a part of my experience and my way of expressing myself. I hope that you enjoy the musical analogies that I include.
- I also have some background in perceptual and cognitive psychology that has certainly helped me to modernized my language in describing my spiritual experience.
- For the past several years Ulla and I have participated in the Radiant Rose Academy, which is a great living source of Ascended Master teachings. We are grateful to Usa for the great inspiration he has provided us.

My effort here has been to work from the heart of what these many spiritual traditions have taught me without appropriating from any of them. I believe that the next stage of human evolution calls on us to move toward a new universal spiritual tradition that is informed by our many individual traditions. We must discover and master our core unity. And it is my belief that humanity is in a process of evolving to a new level of consciousness—to what is often called Unity Consciousness, Christ Consciousness, or 5th-dimensional Consciousness. I hope that this book may provide you with a next step that you need on your path to that higher state of consciousness.

Part I: The Beginning Point

Prelude — An Invitation From Divine Creator

Imagine this: you come home at the end of a long day of work or maybe from running around doing all of your daily errands, and as you enter your home you reach for the mail that has arrived while you were gone. When you examine it, you realize that there is something unusual in the middle of it all. It is a formal invitation in a fancy envelop. As you open it up and read the invitation, you can feel a sense of shock coming over you. It is an invitation to have coffee with Divine Creator. What? A strange hoax? No, something tells you that this is the real thing. You know deep down inside of you that this is indeed a very significant, if unexpected, moment in your life. You can either wake yourself up and respond to it or not. But if you ignore it, you might be missing something really important. And as you look down and read the words that tell you the place and time for the meeting, you realize that you have barely enough time to get there if you leave right now!

Ok. Out the door and down the street you go. You know approximately where you're headed. You look around as you rush past the other people on the street. There is no time for you to talk with them or to explain where you are going. Would anyone believe you anyway? And you begin to wonder to yourself: What should you say to Divine Creator? Given an opportunity like this, what important questions should you ask? What would other people expect you to ask?

As you hurriedly arrive near to the meeting place on the

invitation, you turn a corner and you discover that you are magically transported to a new location. Wow, that was absolute confirmation that this is real! You are now in an open plaza, an intimate, little square, and just up ahead of you is a small, wooden table with two chairs. You walk up to the table, and you see that it is set with the things you might need for a coffee meeting: cups, silverware, small plates, a coffee pot, and even a few scones. Divine Creator seems to know how to set a good table. So, you take your seat and try to look natural and relaxed.

Somewhere up ahead a door opens, and you realize that Divine Creator has just stepped out into the plaza. At first your eyes can't seem to focus on anything as you struggle to 'see' what Divine Creator looks like. Meanwhile, step-by-step Divine Creator walks up, takes the chair opposite to you, and sits down.

And you hear the voice of Divine Creator, "I am so happy that you decided to meet with me. I have been looking forward to this conversation." There is a pause in which you don't know what to do. "Maybe you have some questions?"

Questions? Yes, thoughts race through your mind. What were those questions you were thinking about along the way here?

You manage to stutter a few words, "Suffering, sickness, war, . . .?" Yes, these are the key questions. It always comes down to this: how can such things exist in a world made by a Divine Creator? This is certainly the question that causes people to doubt the existence of Divine Creator. And then, the other question that has been welling up inside of you, the one you were trying to avoid thinking about: "In my life . . .. Why so much . . .?" 'Why so much pain and hardship in my life?' is what you are thinking. You have barely spoken these few words, which have clung to your lips like children afraid of the dark.

You sense that Divine Creator completely understands the questions behind those words you were able to speak.

"Look at your hands," says Divine Creator. "Look closely."

You hold up your hands in front of you, and you stare in some amazement. You have looked at your hands thousands of times, but you have never seen them this way before. It seems as if light is emanating from your palms—the same kind of light that emanates from Divine Creator. You are amazed and disoriented.

"Look really closely into your palms."

You turn your palms directly toward your face to look, and you feel something passing through you. It's the most peculiar sensation. The light from your palms is affecting you, and you are loosing perspective. You glimpse a vision of yourself that you hardly recognize, not you as you are today, but as you might be if you weren't so weighted down. That other 'you' looks so light and transparent.

Divine Creator continues, "And think about what you have created in your life."

A few quick images flash through your mind—moments that really mattered to you: moments of embracing love for your family, the joy of running in the grass when you were a small child, the stubbornness that caused you to become angry and to pass up important opportunities in your life, ... "My life," you whisper to yourself. That does it. You hear a loud rush like wind, and you have this feeling of floating above the space where your body sits. You still recognize the feeling of being yourself, but you—you are seemingly outside of yourself too—looking at your life from the outside.

"My consciousness . . .." The words escape your physical lips without thinking. "I am my consciousness."

And as your body sits there, you see yourself, the table, and everything in a very odd way. You can sense things that you missed before—the unique design of the silverware and the cups, the light breeze blowing through the square. And there is a deep, profound feeling of connection to the beauty of it all. You love this place and this incredible moment that Divine creator is sharing with you. What is that light? Is it compassion? Love? You experience such a profound feeling of acceptance for who you are. So, good question: who are you? There have been so many lives and so many faces. What are you supposed to do with all of this?

All sense of 'holding it together' drifts away as a feeling of boundlessness takes over. You are crying. You are like a bottle that has been uncorked. Emotions simply flow out into the nothingness. It all unfolds like the feeling of a wave rising up and breaking on the beach. You think, "A wave, that is what this has all been—a wave moving across some great sea of possibilities." And in that moment of love and intimate realization, there is Oneness. There is no separation. You are lost. Something is going on, and yet you can't quite hold onto it. It seems as if you are all a blank. And then you are back within yourself sitting at the table with Divine Creator sitting across from you.

"It is the answer to all of your questions," Divine Creator says. There is a long pause during which you realize that Divine Creator believes that you have been given the answers to your questions—if you could just grasp it all. Divine Creator has maybe answered the most profound of all questions. You just can't figure out how to put these pieces together.

As if to give a hint, Divine Creator says, "Your consciousness has been stuck inside some bubbles that you created." There is another pause during which you try to figure out how to connect these words to your experience. "And, of course, as a Creator Being, I want you to feel free to create new and better bubbles now."

You are sitting there in silence. You think to yourself, "What is it exactly that I am supposed to do?"

"Go break some more bubbles," Divine Creator says. "You'll figure out the rest."

You realize after a while that you don't know what else to say. If you can just get your hands around it, think it through, you have been given something very important. So, you stand up from your chair, bow your head in a wordless gesture to

Divine Creator, and turn around to leave.

It takes only a moment to find yourself standing back on the street that you left earlier. You look up at the buildings around you, and you are struck by the details of their architecture, their form and their embellishments—it is as if you are feeling them from inside of yourself. You don't quite know where the thought comes from, but you think to yourself, "These things are also part of Oneness. There is no separation." And you turn to walk down the sidewalk. People are walking past you, all taken up and absorbed with their daily concerns. "They are part of Oneness too."

Chapter 1 — Awakening Oneness

Oneness. It is the single most profound insight that you can ever come to—the thing that could most profoundly transform your sense of yourself and the world around you. Of course, it might also turn your reality upside down and inside out. The deep, beautiful truth is that Oneness is the heart of everything. If you could take a super microscope and peer deep into the inner-substance of the world, into the microstructure of everything that surrounds us, then looking back at you would be Oneness. If you had a super telescope and you could see the borders of the Cosmos, there would be Oneness looking back at you again. Maybe it is only on the edges of our perception that we truly begin to see this. But once you catch a glimpse of this reality, then you can begin to see Oneness looking back at you in everything—Oneness in the grasses and trees, the streams and oceans, the sunlight, and the wind, especially in the faces of the people you see on the street. In the midst of all of the world's diversity with all of its disparities and imbalances, there is this core truth that everything is Oneness; everything emanates the Divine Light of a single source.

And you are Oneness too. Every aspect of your life—your loves, your traumas, and your striving for a better life—everything that you experience is also experienced as part of Oneness. Everything that you have ever done was done in Oneness, because you are the Oneness experiencing the possibilities of your life. There is nothing that is outside the borders of Oneness.

Maybe you are asking yourself, "Yeah, nice words, but . . . What can I actually do with this information?" Maybe you need some time to really absorb the practical implications of this for your life. No matter how removed it all seems right now from the demands and challenges of living in the everyday world, it is indeed an insight that has the power to worm its way into all of your thoughts and to transform your life from the inside. But it may take some time. Maybe by the time you reach the end of this book?

One way to come closer to the actual sense of all this is through contemplating a story. The story that I offer here is one that starts in Oneness with a dream of Divine Creator—a dream in which Divine Creator imagines the billions and billions of possibilities of what could be. The total scope of this dream is way beyond our comprehension—there are so many worlds out there beyond ours and so many different kinds of beings. Divine Creator's great, incredible dream experiment of imagining all possibilities is expressed and projected out through a Cosmos that is essentially infinite. And yet, in this dream we are all playing our individual roles whether we realize it or not.

And imagine the countless possibilities just here among us humans on the Earth: 'What if a human being met their true love?' 'What if a human being were challenged by loss of hope?' 'What if a human being could actually meet Divine Creator?' The many, many questions of 'What if . . .?' are answered over and over again throughout the many systems of stars and planets in an ever-evolving universe. 'What if you came to a new realization about what is really important in your life?' 'What if you became truly aware of who you are?' Just visualize yourself right now as part of Divine Creator's dream of infinite possibilities.

And there we come to the nub of the "Yeah, but . . . ?"—the question that most people think is the big issue with all of this kind of talk. Because if everything is this Oneness, if this is Divine Creator's dream as I say, then how could things have gone so badly? You call *this* Oneness?!? And the questioning can push even deeper, because if this *really* is Oneness, then you personally could never have done anything wrong— because you are Oneness and Oneness is you. There is no 'other' who has ever harmed you, and you have never harmed any 'other.' You were never lost, and you were never separated from Oneness. Everything that you ever thought was a mistake or a failure was also part of Oneness. Maybe you don't recognize this kind of Oneness as the world you experience?

So, we need a story to make sense of the story. You are Oneness, but it is as if your consciousness were held within a kind of bubble, and this bubble keeps you focused in a pattern of separateness that has become the reality you experience. From within that bubble, you may struggle with the issues of your life and you may experience pain. And you may feel isolated and separated from any sense of Oneness with Divine Creator. Lots of things are broken, and bad things do happen. But if you could be transported outside of your bubble, if you could look at your situation from the outside, you could see that your sense of pain and isolation is a local phenomenon, a kind of illusion that the bubble maintains. Looking at your bubble from the outside is a lot like looking at one of those little dioramas that children make, a small world contained in a box, and all of that turmoil and struggle you experience in your life is totally contained inside of that box. So, of course, you want to get on the outside of the box—that means breaking some bubbles.

Path of Healing

We are going to begin a conversation here about your true relationship to Oneness, and we will introduce the 'path of healing' as a way of preparing yourself to experience Oneness in your life. What I want to call 'healing' in its most meaningful sense occurs every time that you break free of the bubbles that keep you locked in limiting patterns of feeling and thinking. In order for you to awaken to Oneness, you need to escape from the illusory reality held within your bubbles. It is then that you will be ready for Oneness.

In general, we might say that healing is a release from any limitations that diminish your readiness for Oneness. And the bubbles that hold you in these limitations have become part of your 'light-body'—that is what we will call the field of all the invisible energies around and through you. Your light-body is your non-physical self. Your bubbles are interwoven in and around your light-body. They are invisible to your eye, and yet they are as real as tables and chairs. Healing a broken leg enables a person to break free of restrictions and to walk freely in new places. Healing your light-body enables your consciousness to break free of its limiting bubbles and to move in new directions. It is through breaking your bubbles that you free your consciousness to explore the space beyond the limited realities held within those bubbles.

We heal ourselves in order to break free of our pains and our restrictions, and also to be open and available to Oneness— that we don't block our own awakening. We heal so that we might create a life for ourselves that expresses our true self and is in harmony with Oneness. There is nothing that informs our process of healing any more deeply than this: Oneness is the beginning and the ending. In between there are a lot of complicated details that shouldn't obstruct the greater truth of our lives. And because our individual consciousness is so tightly bound up with humanity's collective consciousness, this also means our reaching beyond the boundaries of humanity's collective bubbles in order to find a new realm of consciousness for all of us. That too is 'healing'—breaking the bubbles that hold humanity in limitation.

This path of healing ourselves and helping in humanity's healing is a part of Divine Creator's great dream experiment, part of the infinite 'What if?' This healing process challenges you to release the emotional burdens that you carry, your compulsions, your feelings of being ashamed, injured, depressed, and whatever else you have accumulated as a consequence of living in the bubbles of the everyday world. This healing process also guides you to see yourself from outside of the bubbles that have trapped you in thoughts of isolation and sadness. There really aren't any bubbles that can hold you forever. 'What if you learned that you could change what you think you are?' 'What if you realized that you created your own limitations?' 'What if you created bubbles of a different reality, and your consciousness opened up to an infinite universe?'

And at the same time that one part of us may know that all of this is true and that there is indeed a path of healing available to us all right here and right now, another part of us can be stuck in doubt and denial. That part of us may seem to remain isolated and untouched by stories of Oneness and Divine Creator. Every one of us experiences the anxieties of separation and detachment—separated from other people and from the things we want most in our lives. This core feeling of anxiety probably took root early in our lives, and as we grew older the mounting difficulties of our increasingly complex life grew more and more obvious and unavoidable. Deep inside, most people believe that they are trapped in circumstances that cannot be changed. How we come to cope with our anxieties about ourselves and the continuing challenges of our lives helps us to form the very essence of who we are. We create such very inventive coping mechanisms to help us deal with our perceived fears and to explain to ourselves why we can't change our life's situation. Such is life inside the bubbles.

Most of us experience a longing for something that will liberate us and bring our lives into a better alignment with our inner sense of who we are. Those things that we think we need to fulfill ourselves might be just beyond our fingertips, and at the same time we can't get there from inside the bubble. How often we look for solutions and answers from inside the very same bubble that has trapped us! We look for the love and acceptance that our parents could not give us. We cling to flawed relationships that leave us incomplete, and we get other people to tell us what we should do. And the situation is made more difficult by the influence that society's collective bubbles have on our individual experience. Is society as a whole any better at solving its problems than we are individually? Not really. Sometimes it seems that individually and collectively we try to solve our problems by creating more and more bubbles that limit us.

So, how can we both be part of Oneness while simultaneously be caught in a maze of limiting bubbles? We are both in Oneness and in separateness. It is the core paradox of existence: to be and not to be Oneness—to be an agent of Divine Creator's dream, a dream that explores the possibilities of separateness! And ultimately, no matter what path we take in our lives, all paths will lead us back to ourselves and back to finding our relationship to Oneness. Over and over life picks us up, shakes us, and then drops us off back at our own doorstep to start the process again. Whether we realize it or not, we are all on the path of healing ourselves by breaking bubbles—a path that is preparing us to awaken to Oneness.

MEDITATION: I am Oneness

It is a fundamental truth, and it has the power to transform your light-body and change your life—you are Oneness and Oneness is you. Here is a meditative practice that you can incorporate into your spiritual life in any way that most benefits you. It is simple and easily adapted to your situation.

This meditation starts with some initial steps to prepare your space for what follows. The first four steps are a model for meditations and healing practices that will follow later in the book.

1. Close your eyes and sit comfortably.
2. Say out loud or to yourself: "In the name of the Divine Light within me, I ask for a field of Divine Oneness to be placed around and through me."
3. Ask for the presence of your guides and helping spirits who are in alignment and harmony with Oneness.
4. Reach out with your intuitive perception to feel the space of your auric field. Ask that it be made symmetrical and compact.
5. Give all of your attention to your heart area and focus on the Divine Light that you hold within you.
6. As you focus your attention, let that Light expand until it entirely surrounds you.
7. Say out loud or to yourself: "I am Oneness," and bathe yourself in your Divine Light.
8. Repeat the phrase as often as you like and let its impact affect everything that you are.
9. When you are ready, simply open you eyes and stay sensitive to how the meditation has affected you.

Part II: Healing

Chapter 2 — The Path Of Healing

I am a healer. At least, that is what I usually say to people who ask me about what I do. My journey toward becoming a healer started with shamans from Peru. They taught me ways of healing that were deeply intertwined with honoring the Earth and acknowledging the consciousness of all beings of the Earth. Then I continued my studies in Mt. Shasta, California, with the great American healer Amorah Quan Yin, who hugely expanded my knowledge of healing and my technical skill. And I have been a practicing healer for many years, now working in Stockholm, Sweden.

I guess that one way or another I always wanted to be a good person and to be a good influence on the people around me, even if I didn't understand where my good intentions would ultimately lead me. Working as a healer has given a great deal to me—an opportunity to come to a deeper place of understanding of both the people around me and myself. It has helped me to realize how universal are the traps that hold all of us back. It has also shown me how a person's life can be transformed and liberated by changes to their light-body.

It may be a surprise to many people to find out that for many healers like me, the light-body of a human being doesn't look anything like the smooth blend of colors shown in most drawings of the aura or in aura photography. Rather we see the light-body as having a structure and detail that is similar in its complexity to the anatomy of the physical body. Yes, it can have an amazing quality of luminosity and wholeness, but at the same time we can see many specific structures and discrete parts.

I use the word 'see,' but this 'seeing' does not really take place in the physical eyes. This is a kind of intuitive 'seeing' that becomes integrated with the sense of physical sight somehow in the neural pathways of vision. It is a so-called 'sixth sense' that becomes registered in the mind as vision. And, in fact, lots of people have one or more kinds of intuitive senses that are subtly integrated with their physical senses, especially visual, tactile, and auditory senses. For most people, these intuitive senses come through as a kind of subconscious influence that they might not pay much attention to. But exactly what you 'see' depends on the intention that you hold for what you want to see. Most people just don't hold an intention to 'see' anything at all, even though they have the capability of 'seeing.' As a healer, I am always looking for the irregularities in the light-body that most seriously affect my client's wellbeing, and my vision is guided by that intention. So, of course, to me the light-bodies of real people appear quite different from one another, and they are also quite different from the idealized drawings you find in books on healing.

Seeing and sensing in the way that I do, I try to understand the implications and the story behind my client's light-body. I feel its contours. I look for its inner structure. I feel the sadness, joy, anger, and whatever else is held there. A light-body is not a simple thing. It is a complete signature of a person's state of being and their history. And, the nature of the light-body defies common thinking in terms of 3D space and time. For example, all of person's experiences are coded and stored in the light-body. Everything that my client has ever experienced and felt is there in one form or another.

Nothing goes away. In particular, it has structures within it that hold complex behavioral patterns like denial and avoidance. The light-body's various layers can be examined one at a time to reveal the impact of the most difficult events in my client's life. But experiencing a client's light-body is not a logical process of taking things apart. It is more like the light-body sings to me its feelings and its story. Maybe you need to love this music of the light-body to be a healer. To me, it is the music of life's true reality—Divine Light dancing in the form of a human being.

When I am in session with a client, the first thing that I do is to create a sacred space around the two of us so that the client's situation can be experienced from a place of complete neutrality. Then I look to understand what can best be accomplished in the healing session. By the permissions I receive from the client and from the Light Beings who are present during all such work, I am there to act for the benefit of the client. I am given permission to help the client in the ways in which I have been trained. Maybe there is nothing that they couldn't accomplish by their own efforts, but they also have the right to request help—in this case, from a healer like me. I examine their light-body. I untangle the knots. I bind the wounds. Piece by piece I lift up and out the debris that has been deposited over a lifetime. I identify what is stuck and unresolved, and I help it to shift so that my client might evolve and move forward.

The Separations

If there were a single word that touches the heart of what needs healing in every client's light-body, it would be 'separations.' Creating separations is the root act by which we cut off our connection to Oneness and find ourselves captured by bubbles of limitation. Every bubble is like a wall that separates you from Oneness, and your light-body is carrying all of the imprints of your major separations—the loss of a loved one, the abandonment by a friend, the loss of hope that comes from war. And there are lots of small separations that you have accumulated over your lifetime—the belief that you cannot find love, that you cannot achieve your goals, the decision to accept other's beliefs about who you are. Every little separation is like a micro-bubble. Each one holds the limited reality in which the separation made some sense—the misunderstandings, limited perspective, the pain, the fear.

When I view a light-body, I often feel the weight of the separations that my client has taken on. I can feel the hardness of their stuck energies and the tension in their unresolved issues. Quite often the hardest energy that I experience is the result of denial, which is at its core the most intentional and determined kind of separation. Fear is usually the motivation for denial, often it is the fear of facing up to a challenge, possibly because of the belief that facing the fear will lead to some worse outcome. The energies associated with denial (and with the defense mechanisms that are built up around denial) feel to me like solid objects in an otherwise fluid and delicate light-body. Then too, there are some energies that are literally stuck in the past. This is a kind of separation in time that happens when an event or issue could not be resolved when it originally occurred. These energies often appear like ghosts in the light-body, and they can be influencing the client's thinking and feeling even when they came from long ago and the client has no awareness of them. These ghosts will likely keep the client from being fully present in the 'now.'

You are Oneness at the core, but you have separated yourself from Oneness in so many ways. The limits that you imposed on yourself are separations between your potential to be free and open and how you have adapted to the challenges of your life. So many separations at so many levels—so many bubbles of limited reality. This is how the energy in your light-body becomes stuck and immovable. And once these bubbles of separation are entrenched in your light-body, they turn around to become the patterns that take control of your life and hold you in limitation. These patterns become automatic reactions and compulsions. You see, all of the unresolved issues of your life—the deferred decisions, avoided consequences, and insolvable dilemmas—they all add up to affect the overall quality of your on-going life. Everything that is stuck in the past is keeping you from being free in the 'now' and open for Oneness. It is a symphony of energies that expresses your state of being. There is dissonance in separation and harmony in alignment with the Oneness. Your dissonance wants to find its path to harmony.

Self-Knowledge

A key part of helping any person through their healing process is guiding them to awareness and understanding of the issues that are holding them back and keeping them in separation. Self-knowledge is important to knowing how you need to move ahead in your spiritual evolution. Most of the clients who come to me already have been seeking greater clarity about themselves, and most welcome new insights. Maybe they have woken up to the self-realization that they have been controlled by dysfunctional patterns of behavior, and now they want to take back their sovereignty over themselves. Maybe they have experienced some freeing of their consciousness, and now they want more. Maybe they have had one of those key experiences in life when they recognize that they have changed, maybe even by breaking a dysfunctional bubble of self-limitation. One key experience may be enough to light the fires of self-transformation and to reveal the deeper potentials of life. Nearly everyone struggles with questions of how they have come to be the way that they are. We all want to understand how the circumstances of our lives have shaped our identity, and sometimes self-knowledge lifts a great burden off of our shoulders when we realize how well we did with the limited options that were available to us. At other times we might discover the extent to which we have sabotaged ourselves. Self-knowledge is knowing the truth about yourself, and it leads you toward a deeper level of responsibility for yourself. And with that responsibility comes greater potentials for your life.

My first-time clients have helped me to understand how many people believe that they can't change in any fundamental way. They believe that they are trapped in their identity, trapped in their relationships, their jobs, their lifestyle—for the rest of their lives. Often, what they are looking for is relief from the pain of being stuck with no options. We all need to experience that we can indeed change, especially change from the inside out. In fact, we are always in the process of changing. Yes, you can find your way to greater wellbeing—but the path of healing yourself takes time and effort. That is important self-knowledge too.

As you begin your path of healing, it is hard to judge your progress on the basis of your old assumptions of what your life should be like. The more rewarding approach is to simply walk the path of healing and discover where it takes you. Discovery is part of the joy of being on a spiritual path. I know from my experience and from the experiences that others have shared with me that you can never really anticipate where you are heading and how far you have come. Believe me! It doesn't matter whether you are at the beginning of your journey or near the end (so you think!). You can't really anticipate the changes that you haven't come to. So don't try to understand and control how things are going to be. Don't try to evaluate or reason it out. Let it all go and give yourself over to the freedom and the joy, because awakening to Oneness only comes in its own spontaneous way.

Chapter 3 — Finding Your Path in Today's World

My way of looking at people and life is certainly that of a healer, but I have come to struggle at times with that word 'healer.' There are so many associations with that word that almost immediately obscure the actual work that I do in a 'healing' session. In the first place, for many people that word suggests that there is 'an illness,' and that is just a non-starter right from the get-go. If it were true that what I treat is an illness, then I think that all of humanity would have to be considered ill. And what a crazy notion that would be: the thing that is fundamentally wrong with the world is that everyone is ill. That would certainly answer a lot of questions.

But if we are all ill, it might best be termed what the Peruvian shamans call 'an illness of God.' We are profoundly stuck in this precarious paradox of separation: how can we both be part of Oneness while simultaneously experiencing ourselves as separate and limited? How do we escape our bubbles of separation and bring these seemingly incompatible sides of ourselves into some kind of harmony? For example, how do we harmonize the demands that the outer world places on us with our inner vision of ourselves and still be authentic and honest about who we are? How do we become our true selves? You would be quite right to say that learning to live in this kind of harmony could be quite challenging—maybe impossible. It takes a lot of creativity to even attempt it! And maybe that is a good vantage point for understanding the job of a healer: the healer works to accelerate a process of personal evolution by helping to release limiting bubbles and to bring the client closer to a state of balance and harmony with their true self, and thereby . . .

. . . to also aid humanity's evolution. Maybe you feel like many other people do that we have entered into a new era that calls on us all to evolve. It also awakens a connection to our ancient past, a past holding some deep mysteries about our true history. Healing ourselves today is connected to healing the issues of our past. And at the same time the accelerated pace of evolution today is unlike anything that we experienced before. Maybe the past and the present fuse into one another. It all calls for resolution now. In a strangely ironic sense, you might say that humanity is the victim of its own evolutionary successes: we have evolved to the point of having no time to evolve!

Many healers like me have discovered that the old cycles of karmic learning and release have come to an end. Humanity doesn't have the luxury of eons of time in which to be reborn over and over while slowly learning how to break the dysfunctional bubbles with which we have oppressed ourselves. We are pushed to change quickly now. Our relationship with the Earth must change. Our ways of living in relationship with one another must change. All of humanity is facing this challenge of rapid spiritual evolution. Old bubbles must be broken and new bubbles created. We must take a quantum leap into a new way of living—living in closer harmony with Oneness.

I would say that this clarifies the challenge of a healer's work pretty well: assisting humanity to shift from its current state of evolution to the next. Rather than 'healer,' I think that a better descriptor might be 'accelerator of evolution.' I like that description: an accelerator of spiritual evolution and transformation who works with people at the level of their personal lives releasing limitations and activating their true, authentic self. This is something that we all need.

And this level of personal transformation—your personal transformation—is an extremely important part of the global change that is taking place all around us. Your personal evolution is reflected back to you in the evolution of humanity and the Earth, and vice versa. It's more than mere symbolism. The whole and the parts are intimately interconnected: micro-evolution and macro-evolution are part of the same process. You are the world in a microcosm. And that explains what this book on healing is: an accelerator of change and transformation on both the personal and the collective levels. And the key insight being shared here is about how this all comes down to how we break bubbles and how we prepare ourselves to experience Oneness.

Healing the World By Healing Yourself

So, how can your personal evolution be so important that it is connected to the evolution of the whole world? Lets start by examining a small aspect of private life that illustrates this kind of interconnection. It is a small personal transaction that occurs every day, and yet it raises an important spiritual issue that might shift one's perspective and ultimately change one's behavior. After that, we will see how such a personal issue might connect to global consciousness.

As a healer, I think that the single most profound misjudgment that my clients make in their daily lives involves giving away their power. What I mean by that is that one person cedes authority over themselves to another. It is such a quiet, commonplace transaction that it hardly warrants any special notice; in fact, one of its typical hallmarks is that it is not openly acknowledged. For example, a wife might limit her professional horizon because her husband is very insecure about her being more successful than he is. Or a man might not speak out and challenge the prevailing prejudice around him in his workplace because he fears being ostracized by his friends there. In both of these cases, a person has given away a part of themselves. And most of us negotiate our way through life under the unexamined assumption that this is just the way it is: our actions and our identity need to be negotiable, and we obviously need to keep ourselves in check for the sake of the people around us, right? And, of course, the eventual outcome of living life this way is that we mold ourselves into the image of what others want us to be. We sacrifice the power of being our true self in response to the beliefs of others, beliefs that are often part of the limiting judgments of our family, our social groups, and our society as a whole.

These seemingly small everyday situations can be examined through the metaphor of an economic transaction: there is something given and something received, and the agreement to exchange something for something is a lot like a business contract. We might want to ask: What makes entering into such contracts worth the price that we pay for compromising ourselves? We must be receiving something important, something we really want, maybe something that will make us feel safe or something that solves a big problem in our lives. This kind of contract is a full-blown example of a real-life bubble. Lets call it the 'contract bubble.' This bubble holds the meaning of the contract, its context, its motivation, and the feelings behind it—the bubble is a little self-contained reality of its own. And the bubble probably also holds a commitment to avoid looking outside the bubble and viewing its little reality from any other perspective!

In the most typical of our contract negotiations, it is not the reward of a potential positive outcome that motivates the contract; it is the need to avoid a negative outcome—fear of breaking up a relationship, fear of being ostracized by others—fear, fear, fear. Fear presents us with challenging choices, and the most commonly agreed solution is that it is much easier to compromise ourselves than it is to run the risk that our fears turn out to be justified. So, we give away our power, we live in avoidance of what we fear, and we simply 'paper over' our fears with our contracts. For most people the consequence of living this way is that the number of fears just multiplies.

Where are the models that teach us alternative solutions? Is it really worth living our lives in a tangle of contract bubbles and acting as less than we truly are? For example, isn't it possible for a wife to fulfill her highest potential and still be devoted to her relationship with her husband? Maybe the husband's insecurities and misbeliefs need to be challenged by the growth and talents of a beloved partner? Maybe the basis of his fear needs to be faced in the open. In fact, if the wife decides not to challenge the husband's fears and misbeliefs, then she is taking an opportunity for personal growth right away from him. She is making the decision for him that he can't deal with his fears or change his misbeliefs. Suddenly the dynamics seem reversed: the wife's avoidance of her husband's issues is a bit arrogant, don't you think? If it seemed at first that the wife was being victimized by her husband's insecurities, then suddenly the roles of victim and victimizer are reversed. Now, there is a spiritual lesson to behold: the roles of victim and victimizer mirror each other!

All of this really begs the question: What is a healthy relationship? And what is a healthy personal transaction between people? How can we live our lives in a way that does not compromise our ability to be true to ourselves or set us on this slippery slope of victim and victimizer? Can we learn to create healthy bubbles? Lets try to answer these questions through the eyes of a healer, one who can observe the light-body and see how it responds in different situations. A healthy light-body provides a constant flow of energy through and around the physical body, but a healer can also see when the energy is blocked or stuck. This leads us to an important question: What kinds of life choices create these energy blockages and what kinds of choices release them? It is a simple way of reducing the complexity of life's decisions down to the core. The degree to which energy flows in your light-body is a reflection of how well you are living in alignment with your truth. If some decisions block the flow of energy in your light-body, these are bad for you, and if they enhance the flow, these are good for you. What is good for the light-body is good for you—the true and authentic you. There are lots of other ways that you might judge what's positive and what's negative in your life, and these aren't of any use at all if they block the flow of your energy. Your energy is meant to flow.

You might imagine an objection to this line of thinking about the light-body that argues that the complexities of real people's lives are being reduced to a question about energy flow, and isn't that a vast oversimplification? Yes, it is simple. And yet we avoid the obvious, and we give our power away over and over. The result can be seen as blockages in the light-body. The almost obvious conclusion that observation of the light-body ultimately teaches you is that you are here on earth learning to live in alignment with who you genuinely are. There is no way around this.

And that requires some clarification about how you might do that. My healing teacher Amorah Quan Yin said:

"You are here to learn to actively become your own
master in everything. All answers you need are inside
you. All of them."
"Mastery means that you have become the master unto
yourself, with no superiors."
                    — From *Oneness* by Amorah Quan Yin

What does it really mean to "become your own master?" In
one sense it means that no one is a better judge about what is
right for your life than you are. There is no authority on the
true you that supersedes you. It also means that you must
ultimately trust yourself to find the answers that you need.
Your inner knowledge and your inner voice are giving you the
essential feedback that you need, if you can just learn how to
listen. And as a consequence, there is no one to whom to give
your power away. You don't need to compromise your
mastery. In fact, giving your power away is an illusion, because
what you give away never really leaves you. You are simply
living in a bubble where people believe that they can give their
power away, and maybe you have been going along with the
limited reality of that bubble for your whole life. But from a
perspective outside of that bubble, your power never left you.

And in exchange for the power you believe that you give away,
you usually expect something in return. How has that worked
out for you? The truth is that whatever you think you gain—
that leaves you empty-handed for sure. It is like a rigged
currency exchange. The currency you receive in exchange for
your power is usually worthless. For example, giving away your
power in order to avoid confronting something that you fear—
that simply leaves you living in fear! Nothing has happened
other than delaying your recognition and ultimate acceptance
that you need to be your own master. Oh, the delusional
power of living inside such bubbles.

I might add that the only thing in your life that you actually have control over, the only thing that you can truly master, is yourself. When you examine the world around you really closely and you look at things from outside the illusions of your bubbles, you have 100% control over yourself and 0% control over anything else. You might as well focus on making yourself the best that you can possibly be. That is a lesson worth mastering.

Lets reexamine our two earlier examples of giving personal power away through the lens of these observations. So, starting with our wife-husband pair, we can reexamine their situation and view them both as on the path of becoming their own masters. In that case, they can contribute to each other's progress by trusting themselves and in confronting their fears without avoidance. They must have confidence in each other's ability to succeed, because every alternative way of behaving involves making presumptuous decisions for the other person. And our example of the man who holds back from speaking his true beliefs about the prejudice around him, he is avoiding his own growth. However people react to his ideas, his speech is an expression of his truth. Otherwise, he has blocked his own path to mastery. His ideas might also be a stimulus to growth and learning in others. We could say that this man has an obligation to listen to his inner truth and to share his ideas without overreacting to fear, because how is the world to progress if all dialogue is self-censored right from the start?

It is certainly an alternative way of living your life when your starting assumption is that you must be your own master and to be true to yourself in everything that you do. And in your everyday personal transactions you still have the freedom to choose when to give and when to receive, and you can strive to do this without surrendering to fear and without compromising yourself. In fact, this is the only way to live as your true and authentic self: to give and receive without making compromising contracts and to do it from a place of mastery. We are free to contribute to others without a counter-balancing obligation, and we must be free to receive without taking on an obligation in return. It is the only way to have relationships with each other that assist everyone in becoming masters—to encourage the same mastery in others that we embrace for ourselves.

There is no need to judge what is right and wrong with others and no need to take on responsibility for the decisions that others make. View people from a place of neutrality. And neutrality is different from inhibiting yourself from saying anything. True neutrality is liberating. Assume a stance of neutrality toward what you cannot control anyway—you will be liberating yourself.

And there is yet another vantage point from which to examine these kinds of situations. At the beginning of both of our examples, the wife-husband pair and the man withholding his beliefs, these individuals were reacting to their situations from very specific perspectives about what was going on: first, about the roles of husband and wife, and second, about the necessity of group consensus. How did they come to see things in the specific ways that they did? Their situations were not only personal, but could also be viewed in terms of society's collective norms. For example, there are the traditional ideas that a man should be the breadwinner and that a group's beliefs should not be challenged.

These norms are established and sustained through the collective consciousness. Most people think of the collective consciousness as something that is only cultural and is mostly promulgated through schools and media, but lets also consider the possibility that there is also a psychic collective. The power that sustains our limiting interpretations about ourselves, that power is collective—held within collective bubbles. The power of such collective bubbles is reflected in how often people are making limiting decisions like these in everyday life. In fact, the limitations that hold us back as individuals are seldom personal. They are much more often personal echoes of the limitations that are held in our collective consciousness.

It has been said many times that personal politics are global politics. There are so many examples of how the projection of our personal values and belief systems drives conduct on the national and international levels. But it should be clear too that collective belief systems also drive what we might call personal politics. It is a feedback system in which the personal and the collective are interconnected. A personal-level fear of privation drives a national impulse to dominate resources. And a national impulse to avoid scarcity shapes the need of people within the society to accumulate resources. A personal-level fear of the power of women drives a national policy of repression. And a national attitude of repression invites repression into our personal lives.

Imagine now what it might mean if we could live by the model of being our own masters and supporting each other in becoming masters. The personal power with which we enact our personal mastery would enter into the stream of the collective consciousness. We would begin to shift the collective perspective. Just imagine that a model of personal mastery could be projected onto the larger stage of the world. Imagine what the world would be like if nations focused on mastering themselves instead of fearing and controlling other nations. From this point of view we can see that the historical behavior of nations has been a projection of controlling behaviors at the personal level. When these collective beliefs and behaviors change, they would in turn influence the beliefs and behaviors of people at the personal level of their lives. The guiding viewpoint on human relationships given to us through Amorah Quan Yin's idea of self-mastery can change us at both the personal and the global levels.

This Has Already Happened

Without much effort, we can see that the world around us is in transition—to what we can't know for sure. Some potential changes might appear positive to us, while other changes might appear negative. Our cultures, our jobs, our personal lives are all changing and moving in some different direction than we have experienced before. Nothing seems immune to change. The Earth is in transition and shifting toward some new normal where the very configuration of the earth's surface is open to change. Most importantly, the deep, shared collective consciousness of the entire Earth and her peoples is shifting.

And at the same time maybe we know deep inside of us that the future is already here. A whole new way of living on the Earth has already been born and is set loose to guide use now. We have created a collective bubble that holds our vision for the New Earth. For example, we have created a vision of ourselves as a global village, even if the consequences of suddenly discovering that we are all sharing the same home planet are still being worked out. And we have created a vision of a sustainable way of living on the Earth, even if the transition is involving us in conflict and dislocation right now. The collective bubble of our vision of the New Earth is here with us now informing those who embrace it and those who deny it. Our new era has become inevitable. It is just as if it has already happened.

The truth of 'This Has Already Happened' is about understanding that everything is here now in this present moment. Personal transformation and global transformation are interconnected right now. The bubbles that shape and limit human consciousness are both personal and collective. Heal yourself now to heal the whole of humanity.

And if you are searching for a model for how to heal yourself and to heal the world, one can be found in the path of healing. Maybe it is time to incorporate the practices of healing traditions into our everyday lives and then to project these practices onto the world stage. Time to engage this capacity for accelerating human evolution and to use it to guide our evolution. We need more healers—healers in the broadest sense—walking the Earth and preparing the way for Oneness.

Chapter 4 — The Story of Your Light-Body, Part 1

The more that you learn about your light-body, the more likely it is that this knowledge will transform and liberate you from your old notions of who you are, even your old notions of *what* you are. For instance, this knowledge can help you understand how fundamental the connection is between you and Oneness—to understand its significance even for your everyday life. And at the same time, this knowledge provides a context for understanding what 'healing' actually is and what the path of healing can mean for you.

Nearly every book on energetic healing or energy medicine includes some general description of the human light-body, and these descriptions range from ones that are highly idealized and symbolic (like the ancient Vedic pictures) to ones that are more anatomical and pragmatic (like those of Barbara Brennan's books). So, before moving on to talk more about the actual process of healing in the chapters that follow, I want to describe the light-body and to cover some of the same topics that are in these other books. And I also want to contribute some additional perspectives based on my personal experience as a healer. I especially want to share the perspective I have acquired on how dynamic and flexible the light-body is, so that we all don't take what books typically present as something fixed and static. Because as a healer, you observe all of the variations and all the diversity present in the light-bodies of the clients that you meet, and with that experience, you cannot help but appreciate how the light-body adapts to the individual's situation. So, my long-term perspective is that the human light-body has clearly evolved over time and will continue to evolve into the new era.

And for this purpose, I have also decided to tackle the often-perplexing concept of soul and to integrate the soul with our concepts of the light-body. For me as a healer, the soul is not an abstract or theological subject. It is a practical reality for healing. That everyone carries the Divine Light of the soul within themselves is important to understanding the world as it really is. Seeing the Divine Light as a manifestation of the Oneness in the people around us isn't just a poetic idea; it is a reality. It is a starting point for a deeper understanding of life's true significance. To me, the joining of the soul with the physical body is the motivating purpose, the *raison d'être*, for the entire light-body. Without that understanding, I think that descriptions of the light-body can seem pretty arbitrary.

The Mythic Story Of Your Divine Origins

Throughout human history, discussions of soul have been framed in metaphorical language, because metaphor enables us to grasp the intangible in terms of things that are familiar and accessible to our three-dimensional minds. For example, we can discuss the soul and the Divine Light in terms of a mythic story about our divine origins. We can begin our story just as an ancient storyteller would with the words . . .

"Divine Creator began All-That-Is with three ingredients out of which everything in all worlds is made: the blue, the gold and the rose-pink rays. They are more than 'rays' *per se,* because they are the most fundamental building blocks of All-That-Is. They are three components of the original Divine Light—the most pure Divine Essence.

The three rays can be understood in many ways, but here is what they mean in relation to our divine origins. The blue ray is the infinite blank canvas upon which Divine Creator paints everything. It creates the possibility of a space in which something might exist. The property of existing belongs to the gold ray, which appears to us as pure golden light, but it also is like a cloud of fine dust out of which everything is made. And finally, in order for there to be something—anything—there must be an organizing force. The rose-pink ray is the force of Divine Creator's loving intent that gives shape to all things and sets All-That-Is into motion. These are indeed the fundamental building blocks of the universe we inhabit.

The soul originates when a bit of the Divine Essence of the three rays becomes individuated from the rest. First, a small portion of the three rays is scooped out and bounded in space (blue ray). It is still within the Oneness of All-That-Is, but it has also become individuated (gold ray). Then, Divine Creator sets this individuated raw material into motion (rose-pink ray). This individuation of the three rays then possesses both *being-ness*, by virtue of which it exists as part of All-That-Is, and *awareness*, by which it has the capacity to recognize itself and to evolve. The three rays are the nucleus of your divine soul essence and the source of the Divine Light that emanates from within you and from within each and every person."

The 'central character' of our mythic story is the soul—your soul— and the main plot is about the soul's divine birth and journey to join with the physical body. The ultimate 'role' played by the soul is to be an individuated agent of Divine Creator's dream by participating directly in the creative expansion of All-That-Is. The 'setting' of our story is the multidimensional universe of All-That-Is, which is blossoming new potentials like a flower that is opening with many pedals. These pedals include the many levels of the spiritual dimensions. These are not dimensions in the mathematical sense, but individual planes of existence, each separate and yet part of the whole like the petals of this blossoming flower which we call the Cosmos. Those people who are able to experience the different dimensions consciously often describe them as layered one upon the other, each a world with its own spatial and temporal properties. They range from the simplest (first, second, and third dimensions) through the more complex (fourth and fifth dimensions) and on up (sixth dimension and higher).

The Soul Matrix

For your soul's divine essence to be present in any one dimension of All-That-Is (like our world's third dimension), it must be brought into contact with what exists in that level. But by virtue of its pure nature, the divine essence of your soul cannot actually touch the substance of those levels because your soul essence belongs to another level of existence entirely. Our storyteller continues . . .

"Now there must be some kind of boundary between the material world of the body in the third dimension and the pure essence of the soul. From our third-dimensional perspective, that boundary seems like a container. We call it the Soul Matrix. It is the interface between the infinite nature of the pure soul essence and the finite realms of material creation. The Soul Matrix is coupled with the body and yet it is also a doorway to the infinite realms of All-That-Is. It cannot be seen with the physical eyes and yet it radiates forth the pure Divine Light. The soul and the body are joined in the core paradox of our existence—being simultaneously finite and infinite."

A great deal depends on the Soul Matrix. Its geometry is multidimensional and its specific shape determines the particular dimensional level at which your soul is incarnated— 3D or other. This is how each soul is brought into relationship with the material worlds of the many dimensions in order to participate in All-That-Is. The shape and geometry of the Soul Matrix look different at each dimensional level. It is truly multidimensional, and it transcends any comparison to things we know and understand at the third-dimensional level.

The Higher Self

This multidimensional aspect of your Soul Matrix itself reflects the fact that you yourself are multidimensional in a similar way: there is an aspect of you present at every dimensional level through to the infinite space of the Oneness. You may not be aware of your existence at all of these multiple levels, but they are a part of the whole 'you' and a constant presence in everything that you do. We can think of these multiple levels as your identity as it is expressed and manifested through all the dimensions, and we can refer to these collectively as the Higher Self, as distinguished from the 'lower self' that is the limited identity you hold as a physical being.

There are levels of your Higher Self that will always be in close alignment with Oneness—that is their nature. And by their nature, these levels are far outside of time and space as your physical body experiences it. Then there are other levels that are in greater alignment with your identity at the level of your physical incarnation, and they change and develop over time as you evolve spiritually through your many lifetimes. In between these two extremes, time is a kind of sequence without any sense of duration.

Your Soul Matrix holds your Divine Light, and it also holds the unfolding state of your evolution expressed through these many levels of your evolving identity. In this sense, the Higher Self is a projection from within the Soul Matrix and the two are mirrors to each other. From our earthly perspective, they can be experienced as something like the inner and outer manifestations of your divine essence.

The Light-body

The anchoring of your Soul Matrix in your physical body creates and energizes the light-body around you. The very proximity of the pure Soul Essence to the lower-dimensional worlds creates this light-body in response to the power of its presence, and there is a huge amount of potential energy accumulated in the process. The shape of the light-body takes on a very universal form. Its shape is essentially the same as an electromagnetic field—yes, like the field around a magnet. Only in this case, the center of the field is held by the Soul Matrix and its pure Soul Essence, which is an entirely different substance from anything in the physical world.

This field is like a whirlpool of very rapidly spinning energy that surrounds and fills that space of the physical body. And as a whirlpool, it is quite unusual because the energy is actually spinning around clockwise and counterclockwise at the same time. The complementary motions of the energy creates an impression that the light-body is static, when in fact, it is actually flowing dynamically. Energy is also moving in and out of the whirlpool from the top and the bottom of the field. On Earth, the whirlpool aligns itself vertically—with one end open and pointed up toward the Cosmos, and one end open and pointed down toward the Earth. So, the fundamental inception of your life as a human being places you standing at the intersection of Earth and Cosmos, finite and infinite—at the core is simplicity.

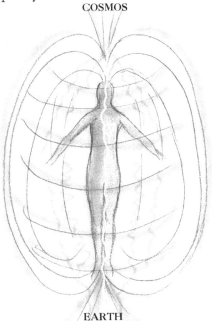

COSMOS

EARTH

For the mathematically minded, we can describe the essential shape of your light-body as a torus, a donut-shape with a hole through the center, except that this hole becomes very narrow as the spinning energy of the light-body adapts to the physical body and anchors itself more deeply. This hole, which can be better described as a tube, is also called the 'tube of light' or the 'central channel,' and it aligns itself with your physical body in the most harmonious way, which is from head to toe in alignment with your spine. And as the light-body spins, energies from the Cosmos and from the Earth are both drawn into the central channel and pass through it. It is a most convenient merger of biological life with the flow of energy from the greater universe.

In truth, the light-body is quite multidimensional and takes on different appearances when viewed at different dimensional levels. Looking closely, the central column can be seen to contain many individual strands of light, each like a thin tube. And at an even higher level, the whole light-body can be seen as a container holding many thin tubes of light arranged in a kind of functional geometry. This is simply an alternative viewpoint on the same multidimensional reality—which is to say that what you see as the light-body is a product of how you look at it. Each perspective can reveal something new and fascinating.

The Plot Thickens: Joining With Biological Consciousness

It is only one of many possibilities that the Soul Matrix should become anchored in a biological life form as it is on Earth. All-That-Is seems filled with unimaginable diversity, and the kind of biological life that we have on Earth is only one possibility. Looking back through the Earth's early history, we could trace how our planet's biology was developed with a great deal of inter-planetary cooperation and cross-pollination from other worlds. It has been a continuously evolving process from the beginning. For example, today's human body has developed from earlier versions of 'human beings' during which the anchoring of the Soul Matrix became established. That means that even very early versions of a human being had access to their Higher Self, not just us latecomers who are the most modern version of a human. All along it has been a process of energetic-biological co-creation and co-evolution. And it still is. The form and structure of a human being is still open to further development! After all, a human being is the expression of the unfolding evolution of the pure Soul Essence seeking to manifest itself within the physical reality of Earth. This evolution starts in the pure essence of the soul, unfolds through the multiple dimensions of the Higher Self, and finds its most individuated expression when it anchors in a biological life form.

Our biological life form has what we can call 'biological consciousness,' which is a product of the brain and the physical senses, which are fixed at the third-dimensional level. At the same time, we have our Higher-Self consciousness, which exists at all dimensional levels including the level of our divine origins. Biological consciousness is a totally separate phenomenon from Higher Self consciousness, even though we commonly use the same word 'consciousness' for both. This is part of the paradox of being simultaneously finite and infinite.

And here is where the plot thickens, because finite biological life forms like us often have a rather poor connection with our Higher-Self consciousness. It depends on many factors, but a very weak connection is one of the many possibilities within All-That-Is. The difficulty of the biological life form to sense the Higher Self can cause the life form to be out of alignment with the Higher Self, and even to experience a kind of separation from Divine Creator and the Oneness—the ultimate individuation. Of course, the biological body and its consciousness are temporal and finite, while the Higher-Self consciousness is largely out-of-time and stretches toward the infinite. So, a core theme in the plot of humanity's story is the complex relationship between your two kinds of consciousness: the biological consciousness and the Higher-Self consciousness.

End of Act I

We have reached the end of Act I in our story. The Soul Matrix with its Divine Light has been anchored in the physical body. And we have been introduced to the challenge created by the joining of Higher-Self consciousness with biological consciousness. From this perspective, we can see that this joining is not just an individual's challenge in life, but also a challenge for all of humanity. And the separation between these two different kinds of consciousness creates a profound need for creative solutions. We create our lives, our cultures, our world—and we especially create our sense of identity—in a constant unfolding process of accommodating a Soul Matrix anchored within a physical body.

Chapter 5 — The Mystery of Being a Creator Being

There must be countless times that you have encountered the expression 'life is a mystery.' In fact, it has become such a cliché that it pops up in all kinds of everyday situations like: 'how to get through rush-hour traffic is a mystery.' Really? It seems that the notion of 'mystery' has become trivialized. But in those unguarded moments when your rational mind's protective shield goes down and your intuitive perceptions are wide open, this insight about the mystery of life can be so pressing and immediate. It is right there on the tip of your mind. And at the same time, it might also feel something quite familiar, maybe a connection back to your ancient past and a reawakening of your deepest feelings for life. When you finally let go of everyday distractions and open yourself up, there is such mystery to life! There is so much for us to experience and to feel beyond the relentless routines of day-to-day modern life. In a moment of expanded awareness, you might get a glimpse of exactly how much lies beyond the boundaries of the ordinary world. Your everyday frames of reference can break down with the sudden awareness that you are indeed walking through life on the edge of a mystery. And at that moment, you are looking from outside the bubbles that hold humanity's consciousness in a kind of hypnotic trance. If you can really take it in, your field of consciousness will be literally expanded by the experience.

There are so many mysteries to observe all around us. One of the mysteries is how so many people are sending and receiving psychic messages while at the same time believing that there is no such thing as psychic messages. Seems that people expect 'psychic messages' to arrive like a post card with some secret clue on it. "The ring that you lost last year is under the carpet!" It is more than a little ironic, because every human being is psychically connected to every other human being and to the entire human collective consciousness. And yet, hardly anyone realizes the extent to which they are caught up in the web of psychic communication. And of course not—because we are all inside of the bubbles that this psychic communication has helped to create!

Creating and maintaining the bubbles that define our everyday reality is the main work of the collective consciousness. We really work hard to hold things together, especially right now during this period of rapid evolution, because this consensus reality is turbulent and quickly changing. Maybe you want to ask, "What consensus?" because it seems that we are all more focused on our differences than our similarities. Just watch the news! Of course, we have all become hypnotized by our global electronic communications, where we are brought face-to-face with one another and all of our differences. But back when we were natural human beings wandering the plains and forests, we were built to hold a consensus reality with our small tribe of hunters and gatherers. We can't do that in the way that we used to before the era of big civilizations. The old conditions that maintained our psychic borders have broken down—that is the truth of our situation. Now we have multiple bubbles of 'consensus reality' at the levels of the family, the tribe, the workplace, the community, the society as a whole, etc. At the psychic level, that means we are confronted with a huge diversity of multiple 'consensus realities.' It becomes harder and harder to stay stuck in the one local 'reality' like the one we grew up in. It appears that humanity is in the process of building a new 'global consensus reality,' but it may be a bumpy ride on the road to getting there.

Creator Beings

There is another mystery that seems truly profound. This one is 'the elephant in the room' that seems impossible to ignore once you know that it is there. This is the mystery of how people can be the creators of their lives and the world around them while at the same time believing that it all came from somewhere else or somebody else. We treat the world around us as if it were just here, like it was delivered to humanity in a package marked "This is the way it is! Sign here _____!" How often does it cross our minds as we excitedly open the package that we sent it to ourselves? There is some huge disconnect between our power to create our world and our recognition of the fact that we have created it. It seems that we have ignored this 'elephant in the room' as a huge collective act of avoidance and denial. And why? Would recognizing it force us to confront some other big mysteries?

We are Creator Beings. That means that we are endowed by Divine Creator with a special capacity and power to create and manifest new possibilities. Manifestation is an inherent aspect of our being the agents of Divine Creator's unfolding dream of creation. It is simply part of our intrinsic nature. We literally create our world, both the visible and the invisible parts. And, of course, I don't mean this in that superficial sense like when people say that having a more positive attitude will improve your life. I really do mean that we have literally created the world around us. To see it clearly maybe you need to look at it from a long-term perspective—from outside the bubble— because we have been at this for eons of time, and working together over many centuries we have rapidly built up quite a complex collective reality, both on the physical and the psychic levels. Do you think that such amazing creativity was just a freak accident by which we sort of avoided doing nothing? Rather, we can make a lot more sense of our history on Earth by thinking of human beings as Divine Creator's 'creative animal.'

And it has to be said that we typically create in a rather unconscious way. We seem ignorant of the extent of our own creative powers. Yes, we probably believe that we each have some small creative capacity, but we seem to have little comprehension of the extent to which it is we who are manifesting the world around us—including all of its problems. The depth to which this insight can shift your perspective is profound, once you grasp how really deep the rabbit hole goes. We are indeed like Alice in Wonderland not realizing that the world she fell into and explored was all her own creation. I am not going to say that 'nothing is really as it seems.' That misses the point. We have created the 'as it seems.' Look around you: we surround ourselves with our creations, and then we act surprised at the trouble we have gotten ourselves into.

A deep truth about the nature of human beings is that our primary way of responding to our challenges and our needs is by creating. We create as a virtually automatic response. We are especially good at going beyond the simple solutions that we need and overachieving. For example, we have created ways of producing food and even turned the preparation of food into an art. We created ways of sheltering ourselves and then went about exploring ways of turning shelter into an artistic expression of form in space. We have created ways of reaching outer space and visiting the depths of the oceans, and now we are turning these those into venues for tourism.

Not to say that all of this creativity always works out so well or produces permanent improvements in our lives. Sometimes it just seems that we are intent on exploring every darn thing that comes into our heads, even some really stupid things. Sometimes too it seems that we are deeply intent on sabotaging ourselves. For along the lengthy path of humanity's creative evolution, we have had plenty of help from other beings who are not members of humanity and not Creator Beings, especially spirits looking to challenge humanity. Many of those have stoked the fires of our fears and fed us a story about how we are not at all the creators of our destiny, but instead the powerless victims of a dangerous universe. When we take that in and believe it, then we become the creators of *their* worlds, often very dark worlds that are actually our own creations. Those lesser beings rely on us to create their worlds; they rely on our gullibility. We are really gullible. Our great spiritual leaders and guides have told us repeatedly that we are divine beings of light, and that we have a special role in the Divine Creator's evolution of All-That-Is. The significance of our being Creator Beings has eluded us over and over again.

Levels of Creating: Third and Fourth Dimensions

We could say that our creative powers manifest on both the micro-level and the macro-levels. Healing is a kind of creative activity that mostly focuses on the micro-level, that is, the bubbles manifested within the light-body. These are essentially structures that individuals have created within themselves. For example, a young boy might receive a psychic message from his father to become more athletic, because the father has unfulfilled fantasies about playing football. In response, the boy might create energetic limitations around his emotionally sensitive side, for example, bubbles that implement requisite patterns of self-limitation. There might be a bubble with a pattern that compels the boy to ignore physical pain, and there might be another bubble that inhibits him from expressing feelings that don't conform to an athletic stereotype. Where do these bubbles come from? The child's focus and intention create them out of the pure energies that are around him. There may or may not be a conscious thought that occurs at the moment of their creation, but there is almost certainly strong feelings that give power to the creation. From

one perspective, we might say that this child is adapting to the parent's idea of who he ought to be, and he molds his energy body into a reflection of the image held in his father's mind. From another perspective, we might say that the child is adapting to living in conformity with his father's bubble.

Another example might be a woman raised by her parents in a religious mythos of transgression and redemption. She experiences disappointments in her life and chooses to believe that it is all her fault because of her misdeeds and transgressions. Her response is to punish herself. She calls to herself energetic beings who assist her in increasing her suffering. They might guide her into creating painful bubbles in her light-body that produce a feeling almost like physical pain for her. She hopes that her suffering will bring about her redemption and improve her life, but she herself has created the mechanisms of her suffering. It is all her own creation. This all makes sense only within her own bubble.

In these two cases, the bubbles of limitation don't exist at the level of third-dimensional reality, that is, the physical world. Neither the boy nor the woman has created a painful physical device in their bodies or changed their physical form. The bubbles they have created exist at the level of fourth-dimensional reality, a level that is invisible to the physical eyes. The third-dimensional plane of consciousness includes our world of solid physical matter, and the fourth-dimensional plane is largely an intangible world that most people only experience indirectly through the significance and meaning of things. We perceive these two planes of consciousness in separate and yet interconnected ways. They both involve structures of pure energy; one is seemingly solid and visible while the other is seemingly ephemeral and invisible. You might say that we are so easily distracted by our physical senses that we miss the ephemeral reality. We like 'things,' and the overt visibility of 'things' on the third-dimensional plane causes us to be so clueless about the fourth-dimensional plane.

For human beings, these two planes of consciousness are totally intertwined: our experience of the three-dimensional world is totally interwoven with our psychic experience of the fourth-dimensional world. A 'tree' is perhaps for us a physical tree, but the significance of 'tree' and its symbolic meaning reside largely on the fourth-dimensional plane in a bubble for 'tree.' In our experience of everyday life, these two aspects of 'tree' are blended together; we can't think about the physical 'tree' without psychically accessing the bubble with the significance of 'tree' that exists on the fourth-dimensional plane. It plays out in how our psychic perceptions are woven into the fabric of everyday reality. If you want to experience the third-dimensional world as a plane of consciousness by itself, try looking at the world while removing all 'significance' and 'meaning' from it. You may discover that you have never really experienced 'the physical world' as it really is.

The great human capacity to create and manifest that we have been discussing here is mainly played out on the fourth-dimensional plane, like those limiting bubbles within the energetic bodies of the young boy and the religious woman. To make the distinction clear: let us say that you think about putting a tree in your backyard. You envision how it should look, and you create an image for yourself of that tree which is full of beauty and vibrant feelings. You are in the act of creating a bubble. That bubble takes on a reality on the fourth-dimensional plane: you have caused dormant energies to organize themselves according to the focus and strength of your intention. But if you want to create the tree on the third-dimensional plane, then you best plant a physical seed. The envisioning and the planting are both acts of creation. But in truth, for human beings these two levels of creation are inseparably joined together. The physical world informs our bubbles, and our bubbles infuse meaning into how we experience the physical world. The two levels of our awareness are so intertwined that much of our fourth-dimensional world mimics the forms and structures of the third-dimensional world. Therefore, the fourth-dimensional bubbles of limitation taken on by the boy and the woman in our examples can easily become conjoined with their physical bodies and then begin to shape the physical surroundings in which they live. Everything is intertwined.

Levels of Creating: the Individual and the Collective

So we understand now that the bubbles we create at the micro-level within our light-bodies lie mostly on the fourth-dimensional plane of reality. At the same time we are cooperating with other people in creating macro-level networks of meanings that are also manifested on the fourth-dimensional plane. Collective consciousness is mostly held on the fourth-dimensional plane where there are piles and piles of bubbles containing patterns of meanings, one inside the other or stuck together, a bit like Russian dolls. Networks of meaning like these are complex structures—structures built out of bubbles.

Metaphorically I could say that we build a whole house of bubbles, and then we live in it. In fact, we build a house, and a village, and a country, etc. We don't live alone in that house, and we have to work together in the creation of a world of meanings that informs our individual lives and which creates a context in which we live together. Part of what makes one group of people distinct from another is the hidden differences in their shared networks of meanings on the fourth-dimensional level. We can communicate with one anther only to the extent that we share bubbles, and missing a few key bubbles can cause a subtle breakdown in communication.

Importantly too, our micro-level bubbles and our macro-level bubbles are tightly coupled together. For example, our micro-level creations could not exist without this larger context of meanings. Consider how the boy trying to fulfill his father's expectations for his life becomes deeply imbedded in a network of images and feelings around sports and its huge cultural significance. And the woman being brought up in a punitive religious family could not imagine punishing herself if the symbolic context and meaning around punishment and redemption did not already exist. In both cases, personal issues are also collective issues.

Being Creator Beings

But what real difference does it make being 'Creator Beings' rather than just ordinary people? On the one hand, can you imagine what life on earth might be like if humans lacked this creative capacity? What would it be like if a flower were simply an object—if it had no meaning in a greater context? An important aspect of humanity is that people fill every corner of their lives with meaning—bubbles, bubbles, everywhere. Humans create these interconnected webs of meaning at every level and within every element of their cultures and societies. The fourth-dimensional plane around humanity is filled to the brim with the bubbles of human meaning. From that perspective, maybe we can begin to understand how significant it is that humans are 'Creator Beings.'

Creator Beings are the instruments by which Divine Creator's impulse to explore the possibilities of creation are made manifest. Creator Beings have a key role in the evolution of the Cosmos. Humanity's creations, some lowly and some high, some anxious and some at peace, all add to the richness and complexity of All-That-Is. We human Creator Beings have created, destroyed, and created again. Over and over. Civilization after civilization. We have created a virtual universe of meaning and expression on the fourth-dimensional plane. We are extremely good at our job!

Conscious Creation

At some point along the path of our evolution, it seems we became so caught up in the distractions and complexities of the world we created that we forgot that we were doing the creating. We enjoy our creations so very much, and that led to our manifestation being unconscious, just happening to us as if in a dream—almost accidental and often quite unfocused. In truth our capacity to manifest with clarity has become substantially degraded by the accumulation of limitations and blockages that we ourselves have created within us. Quite often, at the point when we have decided that we want to manifest something for ourselves, we have already compromised our power to such an extent that our manifestation goes awry. It is not just that we can't manifest a particular thing we want in our lives, we can't manifest anything with much focus at all. Maybe our thoughts and our feelings about the goal of the manifestation are tainted with mixed messages. We want to manifest, but we have mixed feelings about the outcome, and we have contradictory ideas about what it might mean for us. Therefore, when we try to hold the focus and intention to manifest, nothing much happens.

Then too, sometimes our simple intentions to manifest create something much more complex that we had imagined. It is a bit like the creation of art. A painter intends to paint a beautiful field with a distant vista, but the painting also reflects the artist's inner world. The vista dissolves into emptiness, and the field is haunted by huge black birds. Where did all of this come from? Of course, we are unconsciously manifesting things in our lives all of the time. It is just that we maybe manifest things that reflect the disharmony of our inner world. We mis-manifest the world around us and then wonder why everything has turned out so badly.

But our creative manifestations could be something about which we had total conscious control. For human beings to manifest their intentions in the outer world with clarity and authority, they need a level of mastery of their inner world. It takes a purity of heart uncompromised by misgivings to infuse our goals with the power to make things happen. And it also takes a clarity of mind uncompromised by misbeliefs and falsehoods to impart structure to our visions. Manifestation works best when there is clarity of feeling and intention. When our heart and our mind are truly united, we are in the consciousness of unity. To manifest in alignment with our highest good takes a unity. The path of healing is a way to bring us to that state of unity.

As human beings, we possess the capacity to create in a conscious way. We can choose to clear the limitations that we have created, because we know that we created them as divine Creator Beings. We can choose to un-create our cultural systems of limiting beliefs about ourselves, because we know that they have no reality other than what we ourselves put into them. It is time to awaken from our wandering dream and to hold onto this fundamental truth: we are meant to be the conscious creators of ourselves and of our world. And who will we be then when we have come into alignment with our inner truth and turn our powers of creation toward new goals and wonderful inventions?

HEALING PRACTICE: Healing Yourself As a Creator Being

The important purpose for this healing practice is to learn to be your own source of healing—to be your own healing master and by extension to be your own sovereign. As a Creator Being, you have the power to shape and reshape your life, but you need to give energy to the process in order to manifest transformation in your life. This healing practice is a model for some practices that will follow later in the book.

1. Close your eyes, ask for a field of Divine Oneness, ask for the presence of your guides, and balance your auric field just as you did for the first Meditation: I Am Oneness.
2. Visualize in front of you an image of yourself as you are at this exact moment. Feel your true state of being including your challenges and limitations.
3. Place your hands around that image of yourself with your palms facing inward.
4. Ask that an energy run between your hands that gives you whatever you most need to be whole, healed, and in Oneness. Trust the wisdom of your hands to know what you need.
5. Continue the flow of healing energy to yourself as long as you want.
6. When you are ready, simply open you eyes and stay sensitive to how the energy has affected you.

Chapter 6 — The Story of Your Light-Body, Part 2

When we began the story of your light-body, we described how the joining of the Soul Matrix with the physical body gave rise to a field energy around and through the physical body, and we described how its shape resembled an electromagnetic field with energy flowing in and out of the central channel. In this next section, we will explore how the field further adapts to the physical body and how specific structures arise in support of the flow of energy. Just like breathing in and breathing out, the flow of giving and receiving energy is a central point for balance in our lives. This includes the way that energy is moving in and moving out of your chakras and the way that energy is circulated through your meridians and Ka channels.

Adapting to the Body 1: the Chakras

As the flow of energy through the light-body adapts to the organization of the physical body, it takes on greater and greater specificity as the physical body and the light-body become more and more intertwined. Your central channel, which is aligned with the physical spine, is like a river of flowing energy, and your chakras are like the tributaries of that river. It is all like a great river system that has adapted itself to the physical terrain of the body. The energy flowing through your major chakras follows a similar pattern to the central channel and can be seen as smaller whirlpools of energy. Most of them are turned sideways with one end out the front and one out the back of the physical body. And while the whirlpool of each chakra extends outside of the boundaries of the physical body, the real center of the chakra is the hub where the chakra connects to the central channel deep within the body. The dynamics of the whole system is reflected in the fact that at an earlier time, human beings had fewer chakras, and in terms of long-range evolution, we should expect that the organization of the chakras will likely change again. The chakras respond to the needs of the body-energy system. Changes in human consciousness can cause the chakra system to shift, just as a river system shifts in response to changes in the topography of the land.

Each of the major chakras has a unique nature or quality, and one popular way of thinking about the character of the chakras is to relate them to the color spectrum of the rainbow. Rather like the way that a prism splits white light into individual bands of color, the chakras are like color bands split off of the central channel. You can think of the Divine Light of the Soul Matrix as the full-spectrum white light. The crown and the root chakras represent the two ends of the color spectrum— purple and red respectively. Then, the others fall immediately into place: third eye-indigo; throat-blue; heart-green; solar plexus-yellow; sacral-orange.

Add another perspective to this: Cosmic energy is entering the central channel at the crown, and Earth energy is entering from the root. Varying blends of the Earth-Cosmos relationship are mapped along the length of the central channel. From this perspective, we can say that the character of each chakra is determined by where it connects to the central channel along the Cosmos-Earth continuum. The result is that each chakra is like a lens that focuses a distinct quality of our overall consciousness and reflects an aspect of

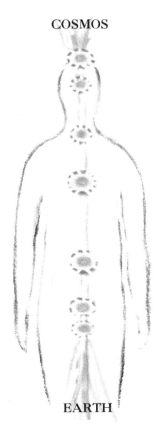

COSMOS

EARTH

our adaptation to physical life expressed along the Cosmos-Earth continuum—very simple.

With the greater specificity of the chakras, also comes their entanglement with the limitations and blockages that we create in our light-bodies. To healers, this is reflected in the great amount of effort that typically goes into clearing these impediments to the free flow of energy through the chakras. These blockages are generally created by conflicts between the Higher Self consciousness of the Soul Matrix and the biological consciousness of the brain. Clearing these blockages in your chakras will also clear the conflicts from your consciousness. Each chakra responds to the conflicts according to its quality of consciousness. Be wary of describing the chakras according to the types of the blockages you find in each. These descriptions are very dependent on culture. A conflict about expressing one's truth might typically manifest as a blockage in the second chakra in one culture and in the third or fifth chakra in another culture. In healing those chakras, the essential goal is reconciling Higher-Self consciousness with the disharmonized creations of biological consciousness.

The association of the chakras with the color spectrum is just a metaphorical way of relating to the chakras, but even a metaphorical system can be useful to healing practitioners who then visualize the healing process in terms of colors. A metaphorical system is a kind of bubble in which the metaphors are a reality. In that way we can understand that any metaphorical healing system can have its advantages and disadvantages. I once had the experience of attending a healing by a Peruvian flutist who associated each chakra with a musical note. The flutist would play for an individual and watch the effect of the notes on the person's chakras. It was a perfectly functional system for clearing chakras even though it was based on a musical metaphor. The metaphorical associations that the healer makes become like magical linkages between our physical world and the world of energy. The flutist's music worked wonderfully well.

The Macro and the Micro

Many minor chakras are manifested in the other parts of the body where the energetic field interconnects strongly with the physical. Each one is part of the symbiosis formed between the light-body and the physical body. These chakras show up in organs, joints, etc., and reading the strength of these chakras is useful to healers because the vitality of the physical body is revealed in the light-body.

There are a few particular chakras that in my experience are particularly important for healing. For example, there are chakras that are above and below the body at the top and the bottom of the boundaries of the light-body. Above the head is the cosmic portal chakra where cosmic energy first enters the central channel. Below the feet is the earth portal chakra where Earth energy first enters. These two chakras anchor the two ends of the central channel. They are both important in healings because significant blockages can occur in each, blockages that limit the individual's ability to take in Cosmic or Earth energies. These blockages may be self-imposed as in the case of individuals who decide to limit the extent of the their spiritual evolution by limiting their intake of cosmic energy, or who try to avoid being on Earth by limiting their intake of earth energy.

In a sense, the essential structure of chakras is repeated over and over again down into the micro organization of the body. Every unit of organization in the body down to the cells themselves generates a field of energy whose shape repeats some variation in the shape of an electromagnetic field moving energy in and out. Really take this in: every cell has its own energy field. And all of the individual fields of energy around the body's parts and systems are interconnected. The whole light-body of a human being is a composite of all of the micro energy fields of the cells, organs, etc. And all of these fields overlap. They all communicate with each other and affect one another. This is how the body functions a whole—micro and macro.

All of these micro fields of energy are in some degree of harmony or disharmony with each other, and an individual's macro and micro energy fields are in alignment or not—often not. In fact, specific energy structures, like specific codes, can be broadcast at one level of the light-body and picked up at another part. For example, an individual's belief in their lack of self-worth can be transmitted to all of the cells whose well-being becomes degraded. A profound deep energy blockage due to a tragic event and anchored in one group of cells can affect the individual's whole sense of well-being. The human light-body is an interconnected system in which there is no separation between the macro and the micro. That is how healing the energy body can easily move between the whole and the parts—there is no separation.

Adapting to the Body 2: The Etheric and Ka Bodies

There are other ways in which the light-body adapts to the flow of energies with the physical body. Besides the chakra system and all of the micro fields of energy, there are two systems that can be described as circulation systems that support the body's absorption and integration of energies that exist above the physical plane. We all understand the physical body's need to take in physical nourishment and to eliminate waste. That need is supported by the body's digestive system. Extend that idea and you can understand the light-body has a similar need in absorbing and releasing energies at many different levels. The chakras are an important system for those processes, but not the only one.

One of these energy systems is the aspect of the energy body described by acupuncture and its related disciplines. This system addresses the flow of Qi, the energy associated with physical life force (also sometimes called Chi or Prana). The major channels for the flow of this energy around the physical body are the meridians. Each meridian channel can be described in terms of its own character and function, usually associated with qualities of the body's internal organs. But at a deeper level each channel embodies important qualities of being that should be in balance to support a healthy life— physically and spiritually. Deficits in the flow of energy in any channel can be related to deficits and imbalances in the whole system.

The Qi channels, both the major meridians and the many smaller branches, are part of what is called the etheric body, the total sum of a range of energies at frequencies that are most tightly coupled with the physical body. The energies of the etheric body are largely in the third-dimensional plane, but outside of the narrow range of light visible to our physical eyes. Even so, these frequencies are so close to the visible light that the outlines of the etheric body can sometimes be seen with the physical eyes when you focus very close to the surface of the skin.

There is another system that draws its energy from the 6th-dimensional plane, and which is a seeming complement to the Qi's connection to the physical plane. It is the Ka body, a system of subtle energy that connects us more directly with our Higher Self. The Ka body has been called our divine double, and it is a central bridge between our physical nature and our Higher Self. It holds qualities and attributes of the Higher Self in a direct relationship to physical life and with our light-body in the 3rd through the 6th dimensions. The Ka body contains a system of channels that move the Ka energy through the body much like the Qi meridian system (with which it is also interconnected). The Ka channels each have their own character and function associated with aspects of our spiritual nature. These channels have themes such as: 'the ability to give and receive nurturing,' 'holding the divine connection in manifestation,' 'alignment with divine will,' and 'remaining balanced in the midst of crisis.' In this way you can understand how the Ka body connects the manifestation of our Higher Self to our physical lives. The more that we live in alignment with our Higher Self, the more the flow of Ka is naturally enhanced. And *vice versa*: increasing the flow of Ka also brings us into better alignment with our Higher Self.

Like the Qi meridian system, everyone has energy flowing through their Ka system, but the flow can be restricted due to limitations we create in ourselves. In the case of the Ka body,

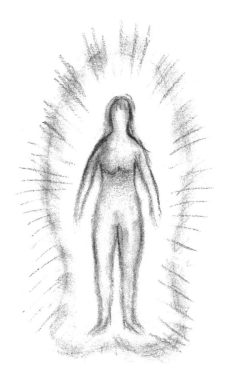

the restrictions have a direct relationship to our spiritual life. For example, a lack of ability to receive as well as to give would be reflected as a restriction in the corresponding Ka channel. In an analogous way to how an acupuncturist can help to open meridians, a trained practitioner can help to open the Ka channels. This kind of knowledge was best understood in the mystery schools of ancient Egypt and earlier. The only modern system for opening Ka channels that I am aware of was established by my healing teacher Amorah Quan Yin, and the techniques are taught today within the Dolphin Star Temple Mystery School.

We are probably all aware that various people have reported the experience of traveling in a light body through other dimensions and visiting remote places. Maybe you have experienced this too! It is often said that this traveling is done in the 'astral body' (to be discussed in a moment), and that is sometimes true. Just as often though, these experiences are actually occurring through the Ka body, especially the kinds of travels that involve flying and ones that are full of light. These experiences are a projection of our Higher Self exploring other parts of creation through the Ka body.

The Conscious-Unconscious Split

Of all the adaptations of the light-body to the physical body, this one is perhaps the most significant reflection of the human condition. There is a special case of a body, like the etheric and Ka bodies, often referred to as the 'astral body.' In my experience people use this term 'astral' in quite a few different ways, and therefore what people mean by 'astral body' is also quite varied. I want to use this term in a very specific way and to view the astral body as filling the gap caused by a separation between humanity's conscious and unconscious. This separation is a by-product of many things we have discussed, such as living day-to-day in bubbles of separation. But maybe the most direct cause is our weak connection to our Higher Self. Maybe too, you could say that it is caused by a uniqueness of our brain structure: so often our one physical brain acts as two separate minds, conscious and unconscious, with a curtain separating them.

To me the astral world is the product of human beings acting as Creator Beings and manifesting from this fundamental split. The astral realms include many negative creations of humans who are often influenced by other beings who use them to expand this space. In any case, the astral world is a transitory realm that will dissolve and dissipate when humanity's consciousness has evolved further toward unity and when the conscious-unconscious split is no more.

End of Act II

This is the end of Act II in our story of the human light-body. We observed how the symbiosis of the physical body with the light-body developed through adaptations. Once they are tightly coupled, changes in the physical body will be reflected in the light-body and *vice versa*. We also come to recognize that the light-body and the physical body are deeply interconnected as a total system. It is no surprise then that the relationship of the physical body to the light-body can be so complex and so dynamic.

MEDITATION: Consciousness of the Chakras

This meditation helps you to fully activate your chakras as centers of consciousness. In this meditation you are asked to focus all of your awareness in the *core of each chakra*—that is the place where the chakra joins the central column. This is the real center, the nucleus, of each chakra. When practicing this meditation, you learn to sense these locations in your body.

In focusing your attention, it is helpful to know that human beings have eight individual points of awareness, and when you intend to focus all of your attention in one place, you are effectively gathering all of these points in one place. If you discover that your mind is holding onto anything else, even in the back of your mind, then there is a point of awareness that is off someplace else. Keep calling all of your the points of awareness back to you until your attention is fully focused in one place.

The experience that you seek here is one in which nothing exists except you and the chakra. In that moment, there is an observer and the observed—you and the chakra. The next step is for you to blend with the chakra, to merge observer and observed, so that there is no separation. You bathe yourself in the light of the chakra, and as a consequence, you amplify the chakra's individual quality of consciousness. There is a description of a similar meditation in Chapter 12 of my first book, *We Are The Future Earth.*

1. Close your eyes, ask for a field of Divine Oneness, ask for the presence of your guides, and balance your auric field

just as you did for the first Meditation: I Am Oneness.

2. Search in the feeling space of your body for the place that is the core of the root chakra.

3. Focus all of your attention there. Observe it as a source of light, as if you are looking at it from very close—as perceiver and perceived.

4. Move closer, blend with the chakra, and become one with it. Say to yourself: "I am my root chakra," and hold that state as long as you like.

5. Have the perceiver take a step back.

6. Search in the feeling space of your body for the next chakra in sequence, the 2nd, the 3rd, the 4th etc. and repeat steps 3 through 5 for that chakra.

7. Continue until you have completed the 7th chakra.

8. When you are ready, simply open you eyes and stay sensitive to what the meditation has opened up.

Chapter 7 — A New Client, Part I

It is 3 pm on a Wednesday, and a new client is about to arrive. Let's call her Ella. Ella comes to me as many often do as a referral from another client. Yesterday I sat down to look at Ella's light-body and to see what kinds of issues would be priorities for today's session. This is what I generally do with every client: I scan their entire light-body well ahead of their scheduled visit, and I make a list of priorities for their healing, because—frankly—I would forget if I didn't write things down. The priorities that emerge will include things that are having the most negative impact on the client, usually blockages in the light-body that really need immediate attention. There might also be dysfunctional behavior patterns that disrupt the client's life: compulsively disregarding their own needs, acting out their own disempowerment, avoiding areas of conflict, etc. Each and everything has its own reason for being, its boundaries, and its content. Each is a kind of bubble holding an alternative reality that maintains the dysfunction. There could be any number of these bubbles that must be cleared before we move on to the other, potentially deeper issues, the larger bubbles. These priorities will be the starting point for the healing session.

When I sit down to examine Ella's light-body, the first thing that strikes me is her emotional contours—her depression, her anger, and her gutsy spirit. Then I systematically examine the inner structure of her field looking at it from one perspective and then from another, and I ask each time if there are any priorities for this healing session. If there are, then I might see something in the light-body that is 'lit up' as if a spotlight is focused on it. I might also just 'know' that something is crying out for help. As I focus my attention on each issue, it is as if I enter inside the bubble of the issue to experience the information and feelings that reveal themselves there.

In general, I might start off by looking at the light-body as a whole, the entire auric field seen holistically. From this I get an overall reading of the client's state of being, and sometimes conditions show up that require immediate attention like overwhelming amounts of foreign energy, collapsed boundaries, or de-synchronized energies. I see that Ella has a great deal of foreign energy in her field and weak boundaries. During the session, I will certainly remove the foreign energy, and as I proceed I will search for the background to the weak boundaries.

Then, I move on to the physical; I ask if there are any issues with Ella's physical body, especially the internal organs. I ask this first because, if there are any physical ailments affecting Ella, I want to catch those immediately. Physical ailments are often a result of long-standing blockages in the light-body, and releasing the blockages may be important to sustaining physical health. Then, I ask if there are any priorities with her chakras. Well, for a brand new client the answer to that question is almost certainly a 'yes.' I will glance up through her seven primary chakras starting with the root chakra. If there is a priority issue in any one of the chakras, it will reveal itself. There will likely be other issues manifested in the chakras, but I will focus only on the ones that are revealed to me as priorities—and right now whatever is happening with Ella's root chakra appears to be work for another day. Ella's second chakra though is quite lit up, both in the front and in the back. There is damage to the front of this chakra and dark energy clouding the back. I sense right away that issues with Ella's father are held in a bubble here. His need for domination during Ella's early life caused her second chakra to collapse in front, and the back of the chakra is full of the repressed resentment and anger that she has felt in response, but never had the opportunity to express. Her third chakra is somewhat frozen, but not a priority for today. The heart chakra is largely closed up, probably as a defense against her family's mixed messages of love and control. Not for today. The throat chakra is lit up. It is weak, losing energy, and structurally misshapen. It seems that her inability to express her inner truth has been playing havoc with her life. I am guessing that she is trying to get through her life by placating others and avoiding conflict, like she had to do in her family situation. Looking at the third-eye chakra, I see that it has an energetic structure over the front of it that is intended to control and distort her view of the world. Both parents were involved in this, and they tried very hard to paint a rosy picture and to hide the real situation that existed between them. This local structure in her third eye is a bubble of a false reality. It is a structure that I can remove easily, so I will add this to my list of priorities. The crown chakra is clearly not for this session.

Now I will scan through the higher bodies. I ask about each of these in succession. I can tell that there are issues here, but as happens with most new clients, the astral body is the one that is lit up for immediate work. In my experience, the astral body is quite important to the client because they can 'feel' their astral bodies in a way that overlaps the sensations of their physical body. In fact, damage to the astral body is often experienced as phantom injuries or pains in the physical body. A quick glance shows me that there is the energy of other consciousness around her astral body—the consciousness of three separate individuals, each of whom is a fragmentary projection of a complete consciousness from another place and maybe from another time. Each is a bubble that holds the meaning and background of why that consciousness is present. Healers usually call these 'entities.' I know that I will have to help remove the energy of each of them individually, but I think that I will wait for the session before looking more deeply into who or what they are.

I check now what I call the dimensional bodies, that is, the client's light-body as seen from the viewpoint of the individual planes of consciousness. I ask if any have priorities. If the answer is yes, I will scan each dimensional level to see what the priority is. And for a first healing session, it is almost always the fourth-dimensional body. Looking at Ella's light-body from this perspective, I see a version of Ella submerged in bubbles that hold events from her early life that still have strong psychic power over her: feelings of intense loneliness, moments of shock, beliefs that reinforce her pain, etc. And there is so much sense of urgency here—a sure sign of influences that disturb her life. The fourth-dimensional body will need attention, but it will have to wait for another session. For whatever reason, it is not lit up for this day's work. No matter how much I want to help Ella by working here, my guidance is that other things need to be cleared before what I see here. I shouldn't and I won't—

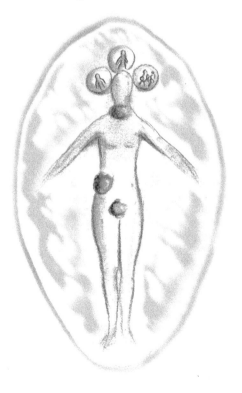

not today—I just trust.

I ask now if there are any other specific places in Ella's light-body that are priorities for this session. I see a spot on her right hip. There is a bubble of dark energy there that is organized around the message "Submit and stay weak!" There are some old-fashion ideas held here that women should submit to the judgment of men and that they need to be weak in order to be feminine. It is another bubble of somebody else's reality embedded within Ella's light-body. I need to dissolve this. I will add it to my list of priorities.

By now my list has certainly grown long enough to fill one session, and Ella's story is beginning to emerge for me. Her parents are very present in her light-body. My impression of her father is that he was a very inflexible man who unconsciously projected many of his needs onto Ella. Ella's mother had withdrawn and was not very accessible, and therefore the father in many ways looked to young Ella to help fulfill his life, but only in the narrow ways that fit his needs. Ella had to repeatedly adapt herself to get her father's approval, as well as to avoid his anger. I don't see any brothers around Ella, but I do see younger sisters. As the oldest child my feeling is that a great deal of pressure was put onto Ella to fulfill her father's drive for the family to be successful as he defined it. He might have been happier with a son, so Ella had to substitute. Ella's mother was rather passive, not because it was her natural way of being, but because it was a tradition passed down through many generations that women were supposed to be passive in the family and serve the needs of men. She was cut off from her own needs.

Ella is actually a product of two family legacies: her mother's passivity which led her to be easily dominated by the father, and her father's overbearing message that the family depends on her, the oldest child, even if she is female. That legacy was born of countless generations of hard-working farmers who survived because everyone had to be subservient to the needs of the family as a whole. Here we are in the 21st century in an urban world of rapid communication, and Ella is carrying around psychological programming from an era of tough rural farming and village life. But it is not just the old cultural programming that maintains this. It is also the way that these traditions and patterns are woven into her light-body. Her father and her mother are not just memories; bubbles holding the patterns of their consciousness are present in her field. Her ancestors are not just people that she has heard about. Their consciousness is alive and pressing their influence in her light-body.

I think that it is important for me to say that this is, in fact, the way things really are with most people. So many people want to believe that there is nothing affecting their lives that they can't see and that there are no spirits out there influencing them—like only primitive people believe. Maybe we are modern people, but we may have more to learn from our ancestors than we think!

I have my list of priorities for the healing session, but before I get started I have to figure out the best order in which to introduce each of these. I will need to explain the nature of the healing process to Ella while I also engage her in a discussion of how things in her light-body could be influencing her life. At this point, I don't even know why Ella has asked for a session. All I can guess is that she has some openness to the idea of healing the light-body because arranging this session was suggested to her by another client. My experience with first-time clients is that some of them are urgently seeking help, while others are searching for something that seems missing in their lives. Some are open and ready to change, while others are protective and want to be nudged.

The doorbell rings. When I answer the door, I see Ella for the first time. She is friendly and just a little nervous. Maybe she is not sure what she has gotten herself into! Our greetings are straightforward as I try to reassure her and to welcome her into my healing space. I want to make sure that she feels a sense of safety here. She has just come directly from work, and I can tell that she is still a bit geared up with energy from the office. We take our places in the healing room. There is a place on the sofa for her to sit. I sit in an easy chair across from her.

I ask her why she asked for a session.

Ella: "I talked with Marie about her sessions, and she spoke glowingly about how they had helped her. She looked really good. She was different. It made me think that maybe I would like to try this for myself."

G: "Have you been involved with spiritual work before? Have you ever worked with a light-body healer?"

E: "No, I haven't been to a healer, but I started doing yoga regularly, and that has really helped me to feel better about myself and to calm myself down a bit. I didn't really understand everything that Marie talked about, but I think I got the general idea of it."

G: "I need to ask a little something about how much you might know about the light-body. Have you worked with your central column and your chakras?"

E: "Oh yes. We did a lot of deep breathing exercises and brought energy in through the chakras. But I think that I could benefit from knowing a lot more."

G: "That's good. And are there any significant events that have happened in your life recently that might be useful for me to know about?"

E: "Well, yeah. I broke up with my boyfriend a few months ago. I was not very happy in that relationship. I had gotten stuck. I had gotten more and more unhappy with myself, and until I was feeling bad all of the time. I had to leave it. Other than that, I don't think that anything else significant has happened."

G: "And what do you want to accomplish with this healing?"

E: "I would like to feel better about myself. I don't seem to be able to feel really good about anything that I do. I have a lot of negative thoughts. Yeah, I just want to feel better."

G: "Ok, I will try to help you with that. So, let me explain how a session is typically organized. First, I will set space. That means that I will ask for fields of energy to be placed around us. The idea here is to create a space whose energy is as clean as it can possibly be—like creating a perfectly clean operating room for the spirit. It insures that nothing comes in that isn't 100 percent light and love. Then I will call in guides from the spirit world to watch over our process and to provide assistance. The guides that I call in are ones who are familiar to me in doing this kind of healing. Then, there is a point at which I will ask you to say your full name three times. What this means is that you are giving me your permission to work for your benefit. By divine law, everything we accomplish in the session is then just the same as if you did it yourself."

I want to take a short break from describing the session with Ella to touch on the deeper context behind what is unfolding here. As I learn the facts of Ella's life, I am feeling for the core story underneath of it all, that is, the story of Ella's spiritual evolution in this lifetime. It is probably a story that is like the stories of countless other people. It is a story of how a pure soul took on an identity of limitations. I listen for the feelings underneath of the words. Where are the constrictions and the pains? And in terms of this personality's evolution, what pressures were applied and what sacrifices were made that formed the web of limitations and compulsions that confine this person now? Life's journey so often is a story of how we give ourselves away. I want to be ready to help neutralize the power of those decisions to limit this life any further.

At the same time there is also a story here about how this person's strengths and talents have emerged. How they have found ways to shine forth with their inner light and to create something of beauty in their life. Maybe there are creative coping mechanisms that reflect special capacities; maybe there are passions and loves that have lifted this life over the fence of limitations. Strength so often grows from our wounds. Maybe there is some special inner self-knowledge that also has led to self-healing.

To me, Ella is a divine soul, full of light, who has found herself trapped within an outer self that has been constructed piece-by-piece in response to her early childhood experiences. It is a construction that prevents much of her inner light from coming forth. Her light-body holds many bubbles of issues that are out of harmony with her true self. A first goal for me is to help liberate her from the programming that restricts who she is. This programming may also cause her to feel disempowered, to think negative thoughts, and it probably causes pain and anger that she tries to keep hidden. This immediate goal is to liberate her so as to make more things possible in her life—to create a better life for her. The long-term goal is to open up a space within her for her true self, her Divine Light, to come forth. My experience as a healer has shown me that much of her dysfunctional programming, her pain, and her suppressed anger need to be cleared before the true self can begin to fully emerge. There is a threshold of healing to cross before the outer self is ready to engage something beyond its current reality. Once that threshold is crossed, another process might begin to take hold: a deeper processes of self-healing, self-discovery, and unfolding of the true self.

E: "I understand."

G: "After these preliminaries, I will start telling you about what I see in your light-body or aura. Before you arrived I took a look at your light-body, and I made a list of some things we might work on. Sound ok?"

She gives a 'yes' by nodding her head, and she settles in on the sofa.

G: "So, I will begin to set space." I have been leaning forward. Now I settled back in my chair. Ella closes her eyes.

G: "In the name of the Divine Light within Ella, and in the name of the Divine Light within me, we ask for a field of the most beautiful crystalline sacred geometry to be placed around and through us. We ask for this field of sacred geometry to help bring everything that we are into alignment and harmony with the sacred.

"We ask for a field of the seven-fold flames to be placed around and through us. We ask for a field of the seven-fold flames, the great sacred energies of change and transformation. And by asking for this field of the seven-fold flames we make ourselves available for change in our lives.

"We ask at this time for a field of divine Unity Consciousness. A field of divine unity consciousness to help us step out of all duality thinking and perception, to help us see and experience the unity in all things.

"We ask that the seed of Divine Oneness be planted within us so that our lives blossom in ever greater harmony with Oneness."

"Into this space we ask for the presence of our high-dimensional guides and helping spirits of 100% light and love. We ask you to share your knowledge and understanding with us, and we ask for your assistance with the work that is about to take place."

"We ask for a connection with the collective consciousness of the masters, and we ask for the presence of any and all masters who can be of assistance in this work today.

"And we now ask to be joined in the matrix of all Earth consciousness. We ask you Gaia, Mother Earth, to help us walk the earth in grace and beauty.

"Ella, would you say your full name three times please?"

Ella repeats her full name three times as I continue.

"We ask that all of the work that happens here today be done in accordance with divine law. We ask that it all be done in alignment with divine truth, divine purity, and divine innocence. We ask that it all be done in alignment with divine grace, divine flow, and divine love. So be it."

And the work begins.

Chapter 8 — The Making of Self

"What is it that I am supposed to be?" That is a question that we are often asking ourselves, especially in our early stages of life. And the way in which we answer that question eventually consolidates into the model of ourselves that we carry around with us for the rest of our life. It must be among the very first glimpses of awareness in early life, that there is 'you' and there is the 'others.' And the way that human beings as Creator Beings react to recognizing the gap with the 'others' is by creating the 'self,' a bubble that holds the model of who we are.

You can describe this 'self' as a kind of personal bubble that holds together the behavior patterns and beliefs by which you define your identity. It then also becomes a model by which you evaluate your thoughts and actions. In fact, most people are constantly adjusting their thoughts and actions according to the model in this personal bubble, even if this process of self-monitoring has become totally unconscious. You could say that having a personal bubble that holds your identity like this provides you with special advantages and potential disadvantages. On the one hand, it gives you a practical handle on who you are in your interactions with others, and on the other hand, it limits the range of your options. Most of the time the increased clarity about yourself is an advantage, but there is a disadvantage if your bubble of 'self' becomes inflexible or it becomes deeply out of alignment with your Higher Self.

Answering the key question of 'Who am I?' is an important organizing force in most people's lives. It gives purpose and direction to your everyday life and significance to your relationships with other people. And without that sense of self, you might feel vulnerable and unprotected, especially when facing the unpredictable behaviors of other people. It provides you with security by clarifying how you fit in with everyone else. And without a model of self, you may not know how you are supposed to respond in unexpected situations. A lack of identity can be scary, and it seems that human beings really, really need an internalized model of themselves.

But where does your particular model of self come from? You can probably recognize the influence of your parents; they plant the first seeds of your identity through their own ideas of who you are and their expectations for who you will become. In early life, these seeds are planted by the psychic messages that they send to you, even before your brain is sufficiently developed to digest them. Their messages are naturally a product of their own sense of identity, so their issues of identity often become your issues of identity.

In the course of most people's early development there is a clear core to the model of 'self' that grows from these early seeds, a core that provides a sense of stability throughout your entire life. Additional seeds can be planted, especially during your childhood development. Many of those will grow in harmony with your core and develop in ways that your parents maybe did not anticipate. Then again, some of these newer seeds may be incompatible with your core and will therefore die away. It is a dynamic process of growth and evolution.

And in my experience as a healer, each person's core also contains a characteristic anxiety, something that gets triggered in response to early childhood experiences. It is usually brought on by the stress of not having your needs met. Whether it is physical discomfort that isn't relieved, or love that isn't received, or just the psychic shock caused by the brutality of the world around you, you react to something in the environment around you that becomes a characteristic reaction pattern in you. The feeling of this core anxiety may become so fundamental to your experience of yourself that you can't recognize its presence, even if it is obvious to everybody else. But that core anxiety is often like a persistent itch that needs to be scratched, and trying to avoid that itch very often becomes the impetus that motivates you to try to improve your life.

The Outer Self

As you continue into your adulthood, the model of self you have developed slowly changes and adapts as you learn to take your place in the world. Especially in your teen years, there are others around you who are responding to your emerging identity and sending you psychic messages that reflect their own perspectives. The question of 'Who am I?' is deeply connected to the question of 'What is my relationship to others?' because identity is never really individual; it always expresses your interrelationships with other people. It is a bit as if you were a new book entering a library and trying to find your place on the shelves with the other books.

And as you enter into adulthood, that core question of "What is it that I am supposed to be?" often turns into "What is it that they want me to be?" The messages reinforcing your model of self that you receive verbally and psychically from others can give a more and more definite shape to your bubble of self. That bubble is especially crucial to you because it psychically clarifies for others how they should treat you! It all becomes a kind of feedback system in which the bubble is reinforced more and more as people respond to you according to your bubble.

Clearly, your model of self is much more than simply a concept held in your head. In the first instance, it is a bubble that holds an overall organization that gives shape to who you are. And in the second instance, you effectively build this model deep into your light-body. You sustain and expand your model of self by creating the myriad of micro-bubbles in your light-body that determine your thoughts and behaviors. It is an accumulation of bubbles with beliefs, images, contracts, memories, behavior patterns, etc. Much of it may be limiting and restrictive because it has the purpose of shaping you to match the expectations that have been projected onto you from others and from society as a whole. You might come to think that your sense of self was just there from the beginning, and that you always were the way that you are, but that is a bit of an illusion. It was always evolving in cooperation with others.

Let's call this aspect of you the 'outer self.' It is what you are to the outer world, and for most people, it is the only aspect of their self with which they have clear conscious contact. You might call the 'outer self' a *functional* part of the light-body. 'Having an identity' is a function of living in the everyday world that everyone needs fulfilled. And from the viewpoint of healing, it is often a function that suffers from numerous malfunctions. No one ever said that the sense of identity you grew up with had to be consistent or workable. Every human being grows up with inconsistencies and dysfunctions in their outer self. And the outer self that you have formed during your early life is typically the part of you that needs the most healing.

When the Outer Self Becomes a Box

As you navigate your way through life with all of the elements of you outer self that you have accumulated, it may seem to you that your life's possibilities are already determined for you—like in certain kinds of video games—you experience open doors and impassable walls. You step easily through the open doors, and you stop and turn around when you encounter impassable walls. After exploring all of the space around you for a while, you have probably found all of the walls that hold you back. They define the limits of your outer self's possibilities. The walls effectively become a box that holds you on the inside. For most people that box seems self-evident and permanent. Of course, as Creator Beings you have effectively created the box. And as long as you believe in the box—as long as you are stuck inside this bubble of your own creation—it is unchangeable. Your box-bubble is a reality as long as you accept its limits and stay inside. But could it be that the walls are really not as solid as they first appear? The model of self that we carry around within us is more fluid and flexible than most people believe. It can be changed and shifted in countless ways that cause the box to change shape and to open doorways that lead to new possibilities. The path of healing is about knocking down walls and opening up doorways.

There are some familiar patterns to the boxes that people create—patterns that we all can recognize, even if we don't often discuss these things openly with others. We may sometimes become aware of our own patterns, but we are usually much clearer about other people's patterns. One prominent pattern is the self-deprecating person who is besieged by a lack of self worth. This pattern usually develops in response to actions and psychic messages received from the parents. The parents' patterns of disapproval are replicated in the child's light-body where the outer self repeats them over and over again. Like a virus, a dysfunctional pattern can be transmitted from one person to another, especially from one generation to the next. This 'lack of self worth' is a pattern that nearly every person inherits in some form. Sometimes it can be a significant part of the box limiting the outer self. And sometimes it is focused in just one aspect of the self such as in a 'lack of attractiveness' to other people or in a 'lack of competency' in taking care of the self.

Once such a pattern like this has become embedded in your outer self, it most often takes over your perceptions of 'who am I?' to constantly reinforce that interpretation of your identity. You can only see yourself through the lens of the pattern, so, for example, everything you take in about yourself reflects a 'lack of self worth.' This is the power of bubbles. You can also psychically transmit your belief in your 'lack of self worth' to others, so that they incorporate this belief into their image of your identity, and they then reflect your 'lack of self worth' back to you both in their actions and in their psychic messages.

There are so many other patterns that we can easily recognize. For example, there are multiple patterns built around repressing anger. This is something that might seem beneficial to the society as a whole, but which is actually a dysfunctional pattern in individuals that creates long-term repercussions. In one such pattern, the outer self thinks and perceives in ways that give rise to a feeling of anger, and then it withholds and maintains the anger, even provoking more anger over and over again. This pattern simply stays stuck right there. For example, a person might decline to express their needs to a partner, and then hold onto the anger toward that person because their needs are not being met. And another pattern is based on denial of abuse. It usually starts in childhood by denying the abusive behavior of a parent in the hope of retaining the love and support that one needs. Anger about the abuse is suppressed. Later in life, the outer self is attracted to another relationship that is abusive, and it builds walls to hide the abuse, probably cloaked in hope of love and support. And, of course, the abuse continues and the suppressed anger breaks out.

Being able to recognize patterns of the outer self like these often means looking past outward appearances. In fact, outward appearances can often point in the exact opposite direction from the inner truth. This is the way that a bubble of denial works. Inside the bubble you are trapped in the pattern of denial, and many of the people in your life who could be on the outside of your bubble get drawn in to the denial with you. They fail to see or think outside of the bubble. How is that? They very often have their own patterns of denial, and your pattern may easily fit together with theirs. Maybe you are all victims of one thing or another! Denial is a way that a group can be bound together.

I once had a successful businessman as a client who projected a strong aura of self-assurance and confidence. When first meeting this man, most anyone would think that he was healthy and beyond any reach of healing. He came to me for help with what he described as an issue with his marriage, but that discussion quickly revealed to me how he was consumed with anger toward his family and toward people who were so less competent than he was. His powerful outer self was a facade designed to completely mask his anger and to convince others that he was strong and in control. He had been building this wall throughout his entire life, and it had become a tool of his success. He had built a wall of denial that masqueraded as a fortress of strength. And now he couldn't recognize his anger at all! I learned from him during our sessions that his family was questioning his judgments, and that some people had started avoiding him. So, a potential lesson to take from this is that when people are pushing their identity on you, it is almost always covering its opposite.

Collective Self

Collective patterns of denial can be extremely destructive to societies. Just consider the effects of the collective denial of racism or environmental pollution. And while it may contradict most people's sense of themselves as free individuals, in truth everyone's model of outer self is deeply interwoven with society's collective models. Every identity is a product of collective identity: society's belief systems, shared history, family legacies, group experiences, etc. And especially during your early years, the dynamics of the culture around you are providing the context in which you frame your sense of self—you identify with this and you don't identify with that. Your personal bubble of self is connected to the web of society's bubbles that give a sense of meaning to who you are.

Most dysfunctions of the individual's outer self are rooted in dysfunctions of the collective. The same issues that we don't know how to solve, society has a problem solving too! Problems in relationships between men and women? Yeah, the whole society has that problem. And the collective also holds other kinds of dysfunctional patterns that affect large segments of the population. Fear of physical harm, fear of deprivation, fear of people from different cultures, etc. are generally experienced by an individual as part of the collective pattern. So, healing the 'outer self' is also an act of changing your relationship to the collective. We can think of this as healing the collective, one individual at a time.

Creating an Authentic Self

What does it take for us to have a healthy outer self? Can we be genuinely authentic and true to the essence of who we are in spite of patterns like denial and the power of collective dysfunction? In our daily lives, we typically hear multiple voices speaking to us and trying to advise us: our biological consciousness has a voice, the collective consciousness is speaking to us, and our Higher Self too. They are all influencing the process of shaping and reshaping the outer self, because the outer self is an on-going project with many influences that unfold over a lifetime. The truth is: we are growing and remaking ourselves throughout our entire life and, in fact, over multiple lifetimes! Each of us is absorbing influences and incorporating new possibilities. The self is often trying on new clothes to test what fits best: "What kind of job might be possible for me?" "Will my life move forward in this new relationship?" "After all my trauma, can I truly open my heart to love?"

The outer self of most people in the everyday world is a combination of both expanding potentials and contracting boundaries. Sometimes these two are mixed and blended within each other, sometimes in a complementary way as our outer self takes on greater strength. For instance, limitations can lead to coping mechanisms that develop into sources of strength and competence. An example might be a woman raised in a family in which all of the positive support for success in life is given to the boys. Girls are told to serve the family, not to engage in the business world. But imagine the obvious situation in which this agenda is out of harmony with a woman's inner voice, out of alignment with her authentic self. She might become rebellious and revolt against this restriction. This woman could become extra creative and determined to overcome the family's programming, even if it creates tensions in family relationships and conflicts in her professional life. After her initial programming is cleared from her outer self, then she is able to identify with her strengths as expressions of her true self.

This example teaches us something important about the creative dynamics of the outer self and authenticity—it is impassable walls that are turned into doorways. It is on the borders of the box of the outer self where transformation takes place and new capacities are incorporated that expand the potentials for the outer self. The box was only an illusion the whole time, and only our belief in its permanence gave it power. But first there were limitations. Creativity cooperates with limitation, even relies on limitation to provide a starting point and a frame of reference. Walls become doorways, and coping mechanisms are turned into new strengths.

There is a counterbalance in our lives to all of the limiting influences from the outer world and from the collective. You feel it pushing back against whatever you think or do something that is out of harmony with your Higher Self. It is a potential for expansion and growth of the 'self' in alignment with the Higher Self and in harmony with Oneness. You can feel its influence in everything that you do, even if it seems like only a whisper in your ear, the whisper of the Higher Self speaking your truth to you. All of your potential developments and your potential decisions are experienced as 'in-harmony' or 'in-disharmony' with the inner voice of the Higher-Self emanating from the Divine Light of Oneness within you. But you can make yourself ready to listen.

Maybe the greatest challenge of living in the three-dimensional world as a Creator Being is discovering how to evolve your outer self in a way that is more and more in alignment with your Higher Self. Ultimately, the outer self must find an expression in harmony with both your physical and your divine nature. This is the great creative challenge of being a bridge between the Earth and the Cosmos—to express divinity through creation in the finite world.

Your authentic self is like the inner vision of a work of art trying to express itself through you and to emerge onto the canvas. The physical world provides the paint and canvas on which the work of art is created. The creative vision emerges from the Higher Self in harmony with the deepest aspects of your soul. The two, the physical embodiment and the creative vision, must be conjoined—spiritual purity expressed through physical means. Yes, the outer self is like a work of art, and you are like the artist learning to paint in greater and greater alignment with your inner vision. There is no one right way of doing this. It is an act of creativity. How exactly does one live in the contemporary world in spiritual harmony with one's Higher Self? The answer to that question has to be reinvented over and over again. The answer to that question is constantly evolving as the world of human beings is evolving. This is what Creator Beings do—create in response to challenges and limitations.

HEALING PRACTICE: Healing the Outer Self

This is an extension of healing as a Creator Being. Here the process is focused on limitations of the outer self. It is especially important here for you to shift the vision you hold of yourself from a state of limitation to the most positive and open state that you can imagine. In this way, you automatically shift your perspective outside of the bubble that holds you in limitation in order to break the bubble.

1. Close your eyes, ask for a field of Divine Oneness, ask for the presence of your guides, and balance your auric field.
2. Think of an aspect of yourself in which you have created limitation.
3. Close your eyes and visualize in front of you an image of yourself affected by this limitation. Feel the effect that this limitation has had on you.
4. Place your hands around that image of yourself with your palms facing inward.
5. Ask that an energy run between your hands that gives you whatever you need to dissolve that limitation and the feelings associated with it.
6. And shift your vision of yourself to one liberated and strong. Ask that an energy run between your hands that gives you whatever you need to be that person.
7. Continue the flow of healing energy to yourself. Continue until the limiting feeling goes away and a something new has been created.
8. When you are ready, relax your hands, open your eyes, and stay sensitive to how the work has affected you.

Interlude 1: The Energy Of Unfolding Creation

All of creation is dynamically unfolding—always changing and evolving. And this change is empowered by a special kind of energy. It is yet another aspect of the world around us that we typically pay no attention to, even though it has the most profound influence on the very nature of our lives. This is the energy that holds the potential out of which all change emerges. It is an energy that is always on the verge of manifesting and creating—transforming your potential reality into your manifested reality. It is like the sun rising on a landscape that is being revealed just one bit at a time. It is like an ever-flowing wave moving through the universe and pushing all evolution along in its wake. When you observe how everything in creation is changing and evolving like this, then you can begin to understand the central role that this energy has in propelling change in your life. Perpetual creation is at the heart of Divine Creator's dream of All-That-Is, and there must be something fundamental driving the continuous creation of new possibilities from one moment to the next.

And here is an important revelation: as a Creator Being you are constantly guiding and molding this wave of new possibilities. It is the power by which you manifest and give shape to the future of the world all around you. No matter whether you realize that you are affecting it or not, everything you do is connected to this invisible wave of unfolding potentials. It is an inherent part of being a Creator Being, even if you are never conscious of it. You cannot decide to turn it off and turn it on. Whatever your life's situation, there is no moment at which you are free from affecting the future. If you are stuck in limitation and sadness, you are actively shaping the future. If you are moving into a closer relationship with your Higher Self, then this is shaping the future too. If you didn't have this connection to the energy of unfolding creation, you wouldn't be a human being. Maybe now is the time to wake up to your true nature and to become aware of the impact that you have on everything that is.

This wave of creative potential is always flowing around you. You might ask what exactly is being created by that wave. On the leading edge are structures and patterns that exist in a kind of pre-solid state. They are the prototypes and the blueprints for what could emerge next. And as the wave moves over and through you, the power of the potential energy propels and animates the myriad of possibilities contained in these emerging forms.

These forms undergo manifestation under the influence of Creator Beings—usually quite varied manifestation that brings forth a variety of realizations. It is at this unfolding edge of the wave that certainty and uncertainty are most clearly mixed. For example, will this new species of fish survive? Will this child grow up trapped in patterns of anger? Will the scope of your consciousness expand some more? And who knows what could happen next? Does Divine Creator anticipate the unfolding of the dream? Or does it simply happen? Can you ever make sense of how the universe unfolds one moment to the next? One thing you do know is that as a Creator Being you have a role to play in the flow of creativity that is powered by this wave. We have previously discussed how we as Creator Beings manifest limitations and blockages as bubbles within our light-bodies. To your understanding of these manifestations, we can now add the realization that you manifest all of these bubbles from the same energy of unfolding creation. It is all part of the unfolding dream.

Becoming aware of the energy of unfolding creation can help you to realize just how much your potential for creativity is part of being a human being. Try focusing your powers of observation on the changes going on around you, and at the same time release all of your anticipation of outcomes. You can feel the rush of this potential energy pushing you—feel the wave of new possibilities breaking all around you. Maybe focusing on the impact of this creation energy helps you step out of your finite, three-dimensional fixation on the world around you, to step out of your illusion that things are more or less permanent, and to open yourself up to an awareness of world's dynamism.

Chapter 9 — The Unexpressed

Way back at the very beginning of my training as a healer, it was explained to me that emotions are the glue that holds blockages together in the light-body, and if you want to be effective as a healer, then you need to help your clients to release the emotions that are stuck in their blockages. Well, for me working as a healer today this is still an important part of how I release what holds my clients back. Facts are much easier for us to deal with than the feelings we attach to them. But all emotions have a story behind them, a little narrative that guides us into the emotion over and over again. Thus, many bubbles that are blockages could be described as narrative bubbles. And still, the most difficult obstacle to breaking the bubble is often reluctance to re-visit the emotions invoked by the bubble's narrative that we don't want to feel. In fact, the avoidance of emotions is very often the key to how the bubble became stuck in the first place!

The profound impact of avoiding emotions was made clear to me in a healing session I had with a young client who was trying to come to grips with a family situation that was a bit unique because her family had migrated to this country just before she was born. She was the first child born in the new culture, and from very early on in life, it seemed that the rest of her family was emotionally punishing her for not being like them. For her parents, she was a child who had never experienced the pain that they had lived through, and they thought that she needed more experience of that hard side of life. "She simply expected too much for herself," they thought. The family had created a bubble around her that totally defined who she was and what was wrong with her. She had lived inside of that bubble for so long that she finally held herself all of these beliefs that they had projected onto her. And all during her childhood, she had tried to fit in with her family by accepting these beliefs because they helped her to cope with her family—beliefs like: "Don't do anything to upset the family," "I can't give them any reason to hate me even more," and "Something is wrong with me for not fitting in with them."

These beliefs showed up now in several ways. One way was that they would manifest as part of the active thoughts in her head. To me, they were 'thought-forms' that emerged around her head and clustered together somewhat like a mass of bubbles. The bubbles would change from moment to moment, but they would also group together to form repeated patterns of thinking  that were steered by her negative beliefs. And there were also very persistent blockages in her light-body that appeared like dense masses that were manifestations of her core issues with her family. From these blockages, those beliefs around her head would be constantly reactivated. These were often highly charged with emotional content.

This client's acquired self-hatred had followed her through life like a shadow, the shadow side of a truly affectionate person who also had deep love for the family who didn't seem able to relate to her life. In our healing sessions I had begun working with her to release these feelings and to dissolve the blockages in which they were stuck. There was anger and resentment that she had held onto and which she had never been safe to express. And then, I asked to see all of her unexpressed emotions. What I saw overwhelmed me. I might say that symbolically I saw bags and bags of emotions piled one on top of the other. She was completely submerged and covered up by the emotions she had held back through her entire life. Days later when seeing other clients, I asked to see all of their unexpressed emotions, and what I saw was often quite similar.

Clearing the Unexpressed

And now I understand how important it is for each of us to freely and immediately express the emotions we feel as part of being our true self. Every one of our emotions that is felt and withheld just sticks around. It doesn't go away. Emotions are like a stream of water that should flow quickly and freely out to the sea, and withholding these emotions is like building a dam inside of ourselves. Behind the dam the blocked emotions form a lake, and in the course of living day-after-day and holding back the expression of those emotions, that lake just grows larger and larger. The common-sense belief among people is that emotions just go away when we ignore them, when, in fact they remain within us, trying to express themselves.

These unexpressed emotions are a huge influence on how we experience our lives, even when all the feelings behind the dam are hidden within our unconscious. The kinds of feelings that we choose to block are often lower feelings that we judge to be inappropriate or improper such as sadness, anger, envy, lust, and hate. Here is where the narratives about ourselves come in, because our judgments of what is inappropriate or improper are all part of a story we have created about ourselves—what is wrong with us and what can happen if we should just express what we are feeling. But even feelings of sympathy and love can be held back when we inhibit our natural capacity to express love.

There are times when the pressure of all these unexpressed emotions can build up and suddenly break through to produce behaviors that seem overwrought and completely inappropriate to whatever triggered their release. Because these behaviors aren't really about the trigger; they are about the denied emotions of the past trying to break through and express themselves in the present. No wonder that we are sometimes surprised by how worked-up and emotional we can become about something really unimportant.

And what is the alternative you might ask? What should we do with our 'inappropriate' feelings? First of all, from my healer's perspective, all emotions are appropriate. Whatever we feel, we feel for a reason—we shouldn't judge the reasons—the feelings are already there. That is not to say that we need to act out every emotion that we feel, but we do need to acknowledge our feelings as a part of ourselves—part of who we really are. You can say to yourself: "Yes, I am a human being and I am feeling that!" We need to 'own' these emotions and to feel them completely, because feeling deeply and completely is part of being a fully realized human being. After we own them, honor them, and honor ourselves, we can let these emotions flow out and fade away into the sea of nothingness.

Maybe the most difficult challenge for us comes up when we realize that so much of what we are feeling in the present originates in those unexpressed emotions stuck behind the dam—emotions left unexpressed and unresolved from many years ago, especially left over from our childhoods. Releasing these can have a huge impact on releasing the blockages that hold us back in our lives today. The truth is too that many of the things that are making us unhappy now are actually echoes of the past. If we grew up feeling angry at being ignored by our parents, we will probably find new circumstances in which we are angry at being ignored. If we felt abandoned by the loss of a parent, we will probably feel abandoned over and over again in new circumstances. The unexpressed emotions are always seeking an outlet for expression.

A Mini-Narrative

So, we might want to better understand how unexpressed emotions can build up and gain so much power over us. Lets say that one day my client as a child might have spoken up to express some desire to her parents—who knows, it could have been something as simple as a desire to watch a particular TV show or to dress in a particular way. And reacting from within their own set of cultural limitations and compulsions, her parents respond in judgment. They have their own sense of how to prepare a child for the difficulties of life ahead; certain kinds of shows and certain styles of dress can lead to her being the wrong kind of person and to reflect badly on the family. They tell this child "No!" And what is more, they project strong psychic messages to the child saying she should correct herself and change the way that she is. In that moment, there are potentially many thoughts and feelings that this child might experience. Her reaction might be no more complex than turning around and going back to what she was doing before with no questions and no anxiety. But more likely there would be a feeling of disappointment that was all the more painful because of the urgency of her parents' overreaction. She might be stuck in fear or uncertainty. She doesn't understand their reaction, and the expression of her true self is cutoff. Shame or anger could follow—anger toward her parents and probably anger toward herself for being so stupid as to ask this question. All of these feelings and thoughts are activated and reinforced in that moment when she experiences her parent's denial of her self-expression. And she might also recognize that this kind of situation with her parents has occurred before, and this recognition now becomes a story about her relationship with her parents—a relationship that is charged with anger and shame. A child's imagination is rich, and ideas and feelings often take on the form of a personal mini-narrative that makes sense of the inexplicable workings of the adult world. And in that moment, this mini-narrative becomes an energetic bubble bound together with its underlying emotions. The emotions are the glue that make this bubble strong enough to persist through a lifetime—the mini-narrative and its emotions are always hanging around.

Maybe the situation described above is just a one-off, but maybe for this child-soon-to-be-client, it is also an experience that is repeated over and over, so that the bubble and its mini-narrative become stronger and stronger. The child's concept of her parent's rejection becomes increasingly rigid, and her feelings of frustration and anger seem ever more present in her life. Other related bubbles might cluster together with this one—bubbles about the parents not listening, their anger at her numerous mistakes, the pain of worrying all the time, and on and on. These bubbles and their consequences don't go away. They hang around and gather more energy as they are reinforced by repeated events. Eventually they take over spontaneous thinking; they become virtually automatic thought-forms—better to say 'feeling-thought-forms'—and they are probably superimposed on situations that are totally unrelated. This now becomes an endless trap, because the bubble of this mini-narrative seeks and finds its own reinforcement. Eventually the client is the intolerant one, and she experiences herself as living in a world where no one seems to recognize her for who she really is, even though she has kept her anger and frustration at bay. Importantly, she hides her true self away as she did with her parents and creates an outward façade that seeks to avoid rejection.

Forming the Shadow

There was another major consequence of how my client reacted to her childhood situation. This consequence was born of the emotions that she left unexpressed and their power to influence how she felt. For when she interacted with her parents and siblings, she communicated through her outer self that had adapted to the family's expectations, but she was also experiencing these events within her inner self. When she couldn't express her true feelings to her parents, she expressed them to herself in a kind of inner dialog. That inner dialog often included the conversations with her parents that didn't actually take place—conversations in which she could be angry, nasty, and controlling toward them. It slowly developed into an alternative self, an inner voice which acted like a safety valve, part of the inner world in which she had retained some control and in which she could react to the problems of her everyday life without the negative consequences of acting out her real feelings. As she moved into her twenties and her lifestyle became more independent, she was afraid to experience the consequences of her inner rebellion from her family. She felt that she was already on the edge of being too independent. She knew how the family would receive her greater independence, and the potential pain was too great. You could say that her parent's discipline had achieved its goals. On the outside she was allowed to express her kindness and empathy—her family was open to that—but her outer self could not own up to the fact that her inner self's negative feelings and thoughts were part of who she was. This inner world of anger and resentment was hidden behind the dam because it was unacceptable to her that she could feel that way. She really didn't see this, because consciously she only paid attention to the outer self by which she adapted to her family.

After this client had established a professional life that took her away from her family, this negative inner voice was always talking in her ear and saying nasty things about other people. It was at this stage that she had begun to tackle her inner darkness. She didn't like that part of herself; it wasn't who she really was. It seemed like a voice from somewhere outside of herself that robbed her of the peace that she wanted in her life. She began to bring it forth bit by bit for healing. She was already into that process when I first met her. I give her a lot of credit for beginning this work before her inner darkness effectively took over her life.

Almost all of us know exactly what we mean by our 'inner world.' We recognize it as the realm of our experience that only we ourselves have direct knowledge of. It is a distinct aspect of ourselves that includes feelings and thoughts that are not expressed through the outer self, and the accumulation of all those unexpressed aspects of ourselves can become like another face, an part of ourselves that we keep hidden. My client had developed an inner world that was like a negative image of what she projected into the outer world. It contained all of the aspects of herself that she could not accept and could not show others. It became her 'shadow.'

At the beginning of the previous chapter on the 'The Making Of Self,' we described how people check their thoughts and feelings against the bubble of their constructed self in order to make sure that they are consistent and acceptable. And clearly that process creates many situations in which thoughts or feelings are withheld because they don't fit with the model. So much energy is given over to supporting and defending our model of who we are in the world that, of course, many free and honest expressions emerging from within ourselves end up diverted or repressed. "Free and honest" doesn't mean nice and acceptable. Everything that is not expressed sticks around in the inner self, and as more thoughts and feelings are withheld, a deeper and deeper separation develops between the outer self and the inner self. The inner self can become a distinctly different construction, one that is an unintended by-product of an overly restricted and prescriptive bubble of self.

But the more that we unblock our expression of what we are really feeling, the closer the inner self and the outer self are to each other. What it takes is a lot of self-honesty and an ability to act in alignment with our feelings in spite of fear. Fear is what divides us from ourselves, splits us into two different people, an outer and an inner self—our sunny face and our shadow. And the more that we are honest and immediate in our self-expression, the more opportunity there is to bring our inner and outer self into alignment with each other.

HEALING PRACTICE: Clearing Unexpressed Feelings

This is an extension of healing as a Creator Being and healing the outer self. Here the process is targeted on clearing unexpressed feelings. You can recognize the feelings that are ready to clear by reflecting on what you feel when you are not mentally active and especially observing the feeling that flare up unexpectedly.

1. Close your eyes, ask for a field of Divine Oneness, ask for the presence of your guides, and balance your auric field.
2. Think of a negative feeling that you experience in your life.
3. Close your eyes and visualize in front of you an image of yourself with that feeling. Let yourself experience that feeling as fully as possible.
4. Place your hands around that image of yourself with palms facing inward.
5. Ask that an energy run between your hands that dissolves that feeling and provides you with healing.
6. And shift this vision to one of yourself liberated and strong. Ask that an energy run between your hands that gives you whatever you need to be clear of this feeling.
7. Continue the flow of healing energy to yourself until the feeling is greatly reduced or becomes neutral.
8. When you are ready, relax your hands, open your eyes, and stay sensitive to how the work has affected you.

Chapter 10 — A New Client, Part II

While I was setting the space, Ella has settled herself deeply into the sofa, and she has closed her eyes. I am holding my hands in front of me with my palms toward an image that I see in front of me of Ella's whole light-body.

G: "Ella, the first thing I notice in your light-body is a lot of energy that you have picked up from people around you. I am curious; what kind of a situation do you work in?"

E: "I work in a small promotions company. We organize events for business groups—small conventions, promotional events—things like that.

G: "The energy I see is rather nervous and unsettled. What is the environment like with other people at work?"

E: "Well, yeah. I have to manage a lot of details for the events. I like that. I generally like this job. I like being an assistant to other people, but this place is a little chaotic. There are constant deadlines, and people get a little crazy when the demands pile up."

I am going about now removing this energy that is like a nasty buzz moving all through her field. What I would say is that Ella likes having an agenda that is set by others, and she is good at taking on the needs of the people around her. It is rather a substitute for her knowing what she wants for herself. But she is also drawing a lot of negativity to herself. I am thinking that her work environment is actually a bit toxic. As I clear away more and more of this chaotic energy from her, the rest of her light-body comes into focus. I can see the weak boundaries around her field, but I will come back to those. What is 'lit-up' for me now is the second chakra. When I look at it, I feel terrible loss, and there is this really dramatic music in the back of my head.

G: "Ella, what I would guess from looking at your light-body is that it is difficult for you to feel safe at work when the people around you are being so demanding. There is a lot of energy that is urgent and on-edge. How do you feel at work, especially when a lot of demands are placed on you?"

E: "Yeah, I sometimes get a little panicked and have to breathe hard. But I do like the excitement at work, even if I feel totally depleted when I go home. It is sometimes hard to let go."

G: "Do you feel the tension in any particular part of your body?"

E: Yeah, low in my stomach—like there is a hole here." She shows me with the hand.

G: "I want to work with your second chakra a bit. Maybe you already know this is the chakra that is most associated with your sense of personal power to feel safe in your life. It appears rather weak to me, and I think that by helping to restore its strength, then you will begin to feel stronger in situations like this at work. Changing the chakra will hopefully change the way that you feel. Sound ok?"

Ella nods her agreement again. I am focused on the rear of the second chakra that extends out the back. There is a dense mass of dark energy that totally obstructs the chakra's normal function. I can feel that there are many emotions mixed here. Fear, resentment, and despair are concentrated here and almost turned solid. I visualize a Quantum Transformation Grid (QTG) being placed around the whole area. This QTG is a healing tool that I learned from Amorah Quan Yin that will break up and dissolve the dense energies. I manifest it in Ella's light-body. I hold the intent that the QTG's power increases while I also visualize what a healed chakra structure would look like. I sense that I need something else to help dissolve what are more complex structures of bubbles. There are ideas, beliefs, and memories stuck here that help to hold the mass together. As a healing technique, I make a connection to the consciousness of the Earth's crystals, and I visualize that a crystalline energy begins to run through the bubbles and the dark mass. I know that the QTG and the crystalline energy work in different ways and that the combination is very strong. In a few minutes the back of the second chakra is clear, and its original structure is clearly visible. I hope that this change will have a direct effect on Ella.

I turn my attention now to the front of the chakra. It is almost completely gone. And there is a large piece of foreign energy with a penetrating shape that is stuck right into the front of the chakra's base. It has a purpose, which is to disempower Ella and to superimpose the will of another person over her. I can call this energetic structure a 'device' because it holds a very specific purpose and works in a very specific way. This is contained in a bubble of foreign energy from Ella's father that came in when he was most intent on controlling her and keeping her from drifting away from the family and her obligations. It also came in at a time during which she was very vulnerable and overwhelmed. I think that she has been trying to find a way to relieve this issue by putting herself into situations in which she feels overwhelmed.

I remove the device from Ella's second chakra directly. I can feel the help of those beneficial spirits we call the angels around me.

This is some kind of important step from their point of view—maybe because this device threatened to derail her life's mission. And now we have to repair the structure of the chakra and also remove the pain that is embedded here. I first visualize a QTG to wrap itself around the chakra and to help dissolve the pain. Then I visualize another healing tool, a Ki-QTG, that is intended to rebuild the structure. What I see in the torn places is the microfilaments of light, the Ki, weaving themselves back together. It is like watching a torn cloth repairing itself. At a certain point the angels tell me that I have done enough and that they will continue working while I move on to other things.

G: "Ella, before doing anything else, I want to ask you about your parents, especially about your relationship with your father."

E: "I don't have much contact with my father. We don't get along too well. My parents moved down south. I have visited them a few times, but we don't have a very good relationship. I really don't like how I feel when I am with them."

G: "And when you were growing up, which parent did you feel closer to?"

E: "Oh clearly my dad. We spent a lot of time together. My mom was more busy with the house and taking care of my younger sister who seemed closer to her than me. My dad and I were better connected, and I have some really nice memories of him spending time with me when I was little. It all started to change though about the time I reached high school. He changed. He was angry all of the time, and he yelled at me about every little thing. We had lots of arguments. Looking back I realize that I maybe caused some of this. I got real fucked-up, into drugs and parties for a while, and I moved out to the city to just get away from it all."

I can see that Ella's father had gotten very stressed and hostile. I suspect some kind of drug or alcohol abuse on his part, but I wont bring this up today. And I see now how Ella's internal strength had saved her from a life that she didn't want for herself. Even though she had no conscious understanding of what was going on, she found a way to escape the confining role that her parents had intended for her. In high school she started behaving in a way that her parents interpreted as rebellion. She became an underachiever and an escapist who 'failed her parents' and who could then just drift off and away. She found an escape, but she is still carrying the baggage of the identity of being a failure that she created for herself.

I turn my attention now to look at Ella's astral body. I immediately see three bubbles of consciousness there, 'entities' as we say. The first entity comes from Ella's father, and it is trying to tell her what to do with her life. It is angry and dogmatic. I can also see it squeezing her body in a way that is like physical abuse. I ask Ella if she feels the influence of her father in her everyday thinking and feeling. I explain to her in general terms what it is that I see.

E: "Yeah, I think that I know what you mean. I often hear my father's voice in my head telling me about everything I have done wrong. There is this awful pressure that is exactly what I wanted to get away from when I left home. I couldn't breathe. And at the same time I think that I have my father's sense of high standards in doing work. He gave that to me before things went totally downhill. Maybe that is why I am good at my job."

I ask Ella if she is ready to get away from this kind of negative influence, and she affirms that she is. I want to lead Ella in commanding away this consciousness from her father, but I know that there must be something more holding it in place. What does she need from her parents that would make her stay stuck in their negative influences? Of course, like everyone else, she needs her parents' love and approval, but that approval may never come in the way she needs it. What else is under this? Well, there is also a belief that she is suppose to stay close to the family and to serve its needs. That belief is part of a family legacy that has been passed down to her. Actually there are two pieces of family legacy, the first that as a woman she should hide her personal needs and serve others. The second is that as first-born, she has a particularly strong responsibility to look out for the others in the family. And, of course, we know now that Ella left home relatively early, but her home did not completely leave her. She revolted against all of these influences, and she became a family failure. I bet that her father still lectures her in the hope that she will turn things around and make something of herself as he understands it. She is strongly conflicted between her sense of failure and her striving for something better and to succeed in her life. Something within herself has driven her to try to embrace a different kind of life, but she has been left wounded.

The second entity around the astral body is from her mother. This is the first time her mother has shown up. This fragment of her mother's consciousness urges her to just be passive in order to survive. The deal is: be passive and someone will take care of you. The presence of these two entities, father and mother, must be like voices in Ella's head telling her what to do and criticizing her life.

G: "And can you tell me about your mother?"

E: "I was really angry with her for not protecting me and supporting me. It was as if she gave up on me in High School and ignored me. I am still angry at her."

The third entity in her astral field is an enforcer of the family legacy that comes down from her father's side of the family. He is an old, religious elder who must have had a strong influence some generations back. His consciousness is still influencing Ella.

When I had originally looked at Ella's astral body, these three entities had appeared to me with fully formed bodies. But I know, of course, that they are not fully present here now. What I see is actually a fragment of energy that mimics their behaviors. Seeing them as fully formed is a 'holographic effect' whereby an image of the whole can be generated from just a fragment. These images are only a part of what Ella had experienced as each of her parents. Ella had never met this ancestor, but the structure of the energy had been passed on to her just the same through psychic communication. Like the energy of her parents, this ancestor seemingly had thoughts, ideas, reactions, etc. But it was simply a fragment that carried a specific message.

I tell Ella about what I see in this family elder and what he represents. She can identify with the rigidity of family traditions and beliefs. She has no idea who this might be, but the personality seems a lot like her grandfather on her father's side of the family. I ask her if she is ready to separate herself from that aspect of the family. She responds in the positive.

We need to remove the entity, this fragment of consciousness from her. By Divine Law she has the right to command it away. I prepare the situation by surrounding the entity in a field that isolates it. I give her the words that she repeats:

"In the name of the Divine Light within me,

I command you to leave
my body, my aura, and my hologram,
throughout all time, all space, all dimensions, and all parallel
realities.
I command you to leave now and never to return.
So be it."

I lift the bubble holding the entity out and away from Ella's
light-body, and I hand it over to the angels. They will take the
entity back to its source, the man from which it came, and there
it will be reintegrated. That family ancestor will be responsible
for his own consciousness.

I ask Ella then if she is ready to command away the
consciousness of her father from her light-body. With her
ascent, we command away this pattern of her father's
consciousness, and soon after the pattern of her mother's
consciousness. Ella's astral body itself is terribly bruised and
beaten. I begin the process of clearing the energy that doesn't
belong there and repairing the astral body in much the same
way that I did with the 2nd chakra.

G: "Ella, how would you describe the relationship between your
dad and your mom?"

E: "Well, they were both very dedicated to being parents, but
they seemed to have little going with each other. I realized as I
grew older just how much they didn't really share much or
communicate."

I am working now to dissolve the mass of dark energy on Ella's
right hip. It holds a specific old-fashioned view of the roles of
men and women that has been passed down through the family
heritage. For Ella the message is that women should be
submissive and weak. That potential programming is out of

alignment with Ella's own nature, although it may have influenced her way of passively slipping out of her life with her parents. I disperse the dark mass with crystalline energy.

G: "Can you tell me a little bit more about the break-up with your boyfriend?"

E: "Yeah, it was a bit of a mess. I had so wrapped my life around him and his friends that I felt like I just didn't matter any more. I don't know how it happened, but I became more and more depressed. I couldn't just go on like that. I just kind-a withdrew. It was really my fault."

G: "But it sounds as if something in the relationship was not beneficial for you?"

E: "Not beneficial. That is an interesting way of putting it. Hard to say, but looking back I think that it was all about him and his problems. It put huge emotional demands on me to support him. He just dragged me down to his level. I think that is fair for me to say."

During this discussion, I have been releasing the energy of this old boyfriend from Ella's field. In my perception, he had become virtually addicted to the way Ella was pacifying his despair and taking care of him. He didn't really want to escape his situation; as long as someone was taking care of him, he had a solution that worked well enough. This was his pattern. He didn't have to deal with the underlying causes of his issues.

G: "Ella, the last thing we are going to work with today is your throat chakra. This chakra is associated with self-expression, especially the expression of your true self. This comes up because there seems to be an issue with your expressing to others what you really need. What do you think about that?"

E: "You mean like in my relationship? Yeah, I mean like I don't always know what I want. But I don't want the kind of empty relationship like my parents had. That is one thing I am sure about."

There is a device across the front of the throat chakra that is meant to block Ella's self-expression. As she had entered her teen years, her father didn't want to hear what she had to say. It had been so much easier dealing with her when she was a child. Her mother didn't want to deal openly with her problems and would rather Ella had kept things to herself. I can tell that they became more distant when Ella entered puberty. Then the mother shifted most of her attention to Ella's younger and less problematic sister. Ella is opening up beautifully with me, but it is easy to see that her needs were not heard by her parents, especially after she entered her teen years. And now Ella has difficulty expressing her needs in a relationship, but I think that she is genuinely an open person.

I remove the device in the throat chakra directly, and I use a combination of a QTG and a Ki-QTG to clean and repair the area.

G: "How do you feel?"

E: "Very relaxed. I felt really tense in my stomach for a while but that has gone away."

I have reached the point now that I understand how I will focus on Ella's bubble of self. This bubble holds her sense of herself as a failure. It is the central theme that unites many of the limitations in her light-body, even though this particular theme only developed in her teen years. It is fed by the urgency of her wounds and the unresolved pain that she feels. And it is an identity that might compel her to put herself into situations of failure as she moves ahead in life. At the same time, I have confidence that Ella has the inner strength to rebuild this bubble as we move along.

I visualize that bubble, and I start now to focus on it with the intent to dissolve it. I understand though that this bubble is not just the idea of her being a failure. It is interconnected with all of the limitations and dysfunctional patterns in Ella's light-body, and breaking the bubble will not by itself erase everything connected to it in Ella's light-body. Both the bubble and its supporting structures need to be dealt with together. And in fact, we have already begun the job of breaking the bubble by clearing limitations in the light-body. Right now I have my hands around Ella's bubble and I am commanding it to dissolve as much as is beneficial to her. The angels are here to support this.

G: "We have shifted quite a lot of energy in your light-body today. We have done as much as I think we can do in one session. I think that it will certainly affect how you feel. And you may feel tired for the rest of the day. What are you doing after you leave here today?"

E: "I am going straight home. I don't have anything else planned."

G: "Good. You should just take care of yourself. Do you have any questions before we end this session?"

E: "Yes. What should I expect now? And what can I do to help myself?"

G: "The changes we have made will open up some new avenues for you. These things in your light-body have made it difficult for you to escape old and useless patterns in your life. Changing the light-body takes the power out of those patterns, so that it is easier to make different choices in your life. Your brain still has some of the same old mental patterns, but the energy has gone out of them.

Importantly, you should be aware that you have different choices you can make and you can explore new possibilities. The challenge for you is largely one of finding what you really want for yourself. What is an expression of you that makes you happy and fulfilled? It is a great time in life to be creative about you.

But I also want to be honest. To my vision there is still a lot in your light-body that still inhibits you. I would urge you to continue to work on liberating yourself. You have the drive, and I would also be very happy to continue to help you.

G: "Anything else?"

E: "Hmm. Not right now."

I am thinking about what is likely ahead for Ella. She will be re-building her outer self as her inner strength and creativity come through more and more. And I think that she is so capable of much greater love in her life. She built a strong foundation when she was young, and I believe that the search for an uncontaminated love in her life is what most drove her to leave her boyfriend and to leave the path that her parents had laid down for her. I hope that I get a chance to follow along and to assist her.

G: "So, I want to close by thanking the guides and helping spirits who have assisted us."

I close my eyes and lift my hands upward. "As you have shown your love for us, we return love to you. Receiving love and giving love. Receiving and giving in an endless cycle. So be it."

Part III: Bubbles

Interlude 2: On Consciousness

A human being is like a wave moving upon the surface of the water. In this metaphor, you can think of the water as a manifestation of the body of the Divine Creator. It is the being-ness of Divine Creator. That you as a wave moving upon this water have this body of being-ness is unknowable to you without some spark of awareness. You might say that your awareness is like a reflection of light upon the water that is caught by the edge of the wave, a small reflection of a greater light that itself comes from the awareness of Divine Creator. You have a reflected light that is actually Divine Creator's light. In that moment of reflection upon the water, awareness recognizes itself. And for that moment, the wave with its reflected light seems like a thing unto itself, something that is separate and independent. But its body is made of the water that is Divine Creator's body, and its light is a reflection of Divine Creator's light.

Then what about our consciousness? Both the light and the wave are necessary for a localized consciousness like ours. There must be awareness anchored in being-ness. We have such difficulty with this question of consciousness, because as we move closer and closer to the direct emanation of Divine Creator reflected in us, we loose all ability to describe it from the outside as if we were an observer. We think that consciousness is ours, but it is Divine Creator's. We no more own our consciousness than we own the stars. The consciousness in us simply is. And the greatest thing we can do to open and expand our consciousness is to let go of our ownership and simply flow like the wave. You might say:

"Everything that I am is not mine. My body is not mine. My way of living is not mine. My very consciousness is not mine. Nothing is mine. It is all part of what is—part of Divine Creator's mysterious manifestation."

And as the wave moves across the water, it forms bubbles. This has some important things to tell us about the nature of our consciousness. From our point of view, there appears to be a veil of separation between our consciousness and the consciousness of Divine Creator. But it is the thin film of a bubble that surrounds what that we identify as ourselves. That bubble holds us within the world of time and space as we have come to know it. Outside of that bubble these things do not exist in that way. Outside of that bubble what we imagine ourselves to be does not exist in the sense that we usually experience ourselves.

And then, within that thin bubble of time and space, consciousness has a dual existence. It is eternal, and it also moves through a world of time and space wherein consciousness appears to flow like the motion of a wave. The bubble of time and space itself is filled with many other bubbles that guide the flow of consciousness through patterns that are based in time and space. How can this dual existence be? You could say that this bubble separates the world of time and space from the world outside of that, and even still, Divine Creator's consciousness transcends the barriers of time and space. So from within the bubble of time and space, issues of consciousness are always impossible to fully grasp, because it is impossible for a human being to grasp a world outside of all bubbles. When we leave the bubbles, we are in the boundless body and the light of Divine Creator.

As human beings, we need bubbles. Within the world of time and space, our consciousness needs the focus and definition that bubbles provide, even as our bubbles constantly evolve and we bring our world of time and space into greater and greater harmony with the Oneness that is itself beyond time and space. We live in the finite, and we live in the infinite.

MEDITATION: Gateway to Unity
Consciousness

This meditation is extends methods introduced in the
meditation Consciousness of the Chakras. In this case you work
with only two centers: the center of awareness that is anchored
in the pineal gland in the head and the flame of the Divine
Light anchored in the Soul Matrix. The center of awareness is
often perceived as a sphere of light in the middle of the head,
and the flame of the Divine Light is usually perceived in the
center of the chest, slightly higher than the heart chakra.

You begin by observing each center and then effectively
becoming one with it by remove the separation between the
perceiver to the perceived. In the final step, you merge the two
centers together, which bridges the separation of mind and
heart and thereby helps you to move into Unity Consciousness.
There is a very complete description of this meditation in
Chapter 12 of my first book, *We Are The Future Earth.*

1. Close your eyes, ask for a field of Divine Oneness, ask for
    the presence of your guides, and balance your auric field.
2. Search in the feeling space of your body for the place that is
    the center of awareness anchored in the pineal gland.
3. Focus all of your attention there. Observe it as a ball of
    light, as if you are looking at it from very close—as perceiver
    and perceived. Move closer, blend with it, and become one
    with it. Say to yourself: "I am my center of awareness," and
    hold that state as long as you like.
4. Have the perceiver take a step back.
5. Search in the feeling space of your body for the place that
    holds the flame of your Divine Light.
6. Focus all of your attention there. Observe it as a source of
    light, as if you are looking at it from very close—as perceiver

and perceived. Move closer, blend with it, and become one with it. Say to yourself: "I am the flame of my Divine Light," and hold that state as long as you like.

7. Have the perceiver take a step back.

8. You might want to repeat steps 2 through 6 before proceeding.

9. Observe the two centers and ask that their light come together and be merged into one light. Let go of three-dimensional thinking and discover for yourself how to let this happen. Come closer and blend with this merged light. Absorb yourself in the state of consciousness that this creates. Let this move through everything that you are. Hold it for as long as you like.

10. When you are ready, simply open you eyes and stay sensitive to what the meditation has opened up.

Chapter 11 — Dissociated Consciousness

When you work as a healer, you encounter a number of phenomena that appear at first to be unrelated to one another, but later on they reveal themselves to be all aspects of the very same phenomenon. And that observation in itself reflects something very important about the nature of our reality, and that is how so much apparent diversity is spun out from a few essential forms. The essential form in this case is the bubble and how our consciousness flows through the bubbles that we create as Creator Beings. A lot of our bubbles contain specific patterns of behavior or beliefs. But they can also become so complex that the bubbles appear to us as the consciousness of another person or even a non-physical being. We have already discussed a few of these phenomena. Think back to 'parents in the field,' 'past-life entities,' and 'the shadow'—they all have a few essential things in common. They are all bubbles containing complex patterns of consciousness that exhibit a degree of independence. They all exist on planes of consciousness beyond the three-dimensional world that our bodies inhabit. And they are all examples of what we will call 'dissociated consciousness.'

Unintegrated Child

To this list of examples, let's add another variation of this phenomenon. The most familiar form of this is the unintegrated child. Many of my clients have an aspect of themselves from their childhoods that has gotten separated and detached from themselves. Maybe because of trauma, maybe because it was necessary for the survival of the self, or whatever—there are lots of ways in which this can happen. And it happens fairly frequently with children.

But then, what actually is an unintegrated child? To my eyes what I see in the space of the adult's light-body is a fully formed image of the client as a child. The image can appear complete, but I know that it is a fragment that only appears to be whole due to the 'holographic effect.' So, it is a fragment from the client's childhood consciousness that has become stuck in time and dissociated from the whole. It is caught in a bubble that sustains the context and circumstances of whatever caused this fragment to become separate. The main impact of this separation is that the client and the child are having separate experiences. The child-fragment is experiencing the client's life in terms of the reality inside its own bubble, which is generally trapped in childhood and a place of woundedness. Meanwhile, the client is moving on with their life in isolation from this lost aspect from their childhood. Maybe the client doesn't know how to reach the child's experience. Maybe the client can't allow themself to feel what the child feels because it is too painful or because it brings up issues that the client is not ready to face. When consciousness becomes dissociated during the first three years of life, it can be almost impossible to access. So the bubble of the child's consciousness remains separate and dissociated from the client's conscious awareness. But even if the client is unaware of the unintegrated child, that fragment is experiencing events and reacting to the client's life according to the reality inside of its bubble.

There are two independent reactions going on side-by-side and affecting one another. The adult appears independent and is simultaneously connected to the child and sensing its reactions. For the adult, this will likely be a very strong unconscious influence on the adult's inner world. Maybe the client has these feelings and dreams that seem to come from nowhere and to be out of synch with the client's outer world. The child's presence can also be like a constant backdrop to everything that happens. An unintegrated child who is stuck in fear may create a backdrop of fear that seems quite out of alignment with the client's everyday life. But it might also be that the child has suppressed capacities for compassion and creativity that the adult is missing. The child's capacity for feeling may be walled off from the outer self, which is held back by this unintegrated consciousness. I remember one client whose mother constantly criticized her early artwork. The adult then was quite afraid of any risks in self-expression.

So, what exactly is this child fragment in the light-body? To me, it is at its root a pattern for the flow of consciousness held in a bubble that has gotten stuck in time. It is a pattern that became separated from the client's other patterns of consciousness during childhood and failed to develop any further. It is like a lake that has gotten cut off from the main body of water, but it is still being fed from the same spring. The adult's energy empowers the child fragment, even when the adult can't experience the child's presence in any conscious way.

Ultimately the two patterns of consciousness need to be reunited. The process of reunion could follow along several different paths depending on the cause of the separation. It may be that the child pattern needs something from the adult that it was denied—like love and acceptance. A process of acting out and giving that love and acceptance to the child might be all that is needed for the reintegration to proceed. More often though, the child's original wounds need clearing and cleansing before reintegration can happen. And finally, the adult's light-body also needs to be cleared of whatever motivated this separation, because it happened and it has been maintained for a reason. There must have been some benefit to pushing this fragment of the child away, and whatever beliefs and feelings support that perceived benefit need to be released before the child can be welcomed back without reservation.

Past Lives

To me, past lives can often appear as dissociated consciousness very similarly to the unintegrated child. Most past lives are uncomplicated and are simply recorded as part of the client's soul history. In relation to the client's present life, they can be more-or-less neutral. But past lives with trauma and unresolved issues can have a very profound influence on the client. The most common theme I encounter with these lives is unresolved trauma at the time of death, something in the client that cries out for resolution. In the process of dying, some part of the client's consciousness detaches itself from the rest. War is a common thread to many of these incidents, and one of the unacknowledged legacies of war is the psychic trauma of terrible deaths that is carried on into the light-bodies of subsequent generations in the form of dissociated consciousness. So many times I have worked with a client to heal the loss of meaning and disillusionment they experienced from death in battle. And a similar form of trauma arises from the deaths of innocents who were only trying to survive the war.

Past lives like these often look to me like ghosts in the light-body. They are like phantom images that are in the field and somehow at the same time not in the field. The language I use with myself to describe this is to say that these ghosts are 'out of phase' with the rest of the field. And, of course, they do belong in a different time. Such remnants of the past get carried forward into the present even if they are only like ghosts. I often work to change the phase of these ghosts and to bring them into alignment with the present before proceeding with their healing.

This ghost in the light-body is a bubble with a pattern of consciousness that cries out for resolution. It might be in spiritual pain or bewilderment. And like the unintegrated child, these phantom fragments of past lives can exert a powerful, unconscious influence over the client's 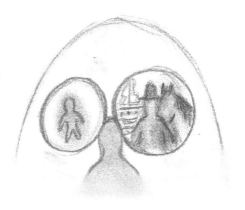 life. My task as healer is to help the client to reintegrate this aspect of themselves, that is, to heal the fragment and then to integrate the bubble of consciousness back into the light-body. An example of a ghost in the field might be the warrior who felt that his god betrayed him by allowing him to die in battle. At the moment of death the warrior is stuck in anger and hatred toward god. Another example of an unresolved death might be a person who was killed by a family member in an act of jealousy. In that moment when a potential life is stolen away in an act of betrayal, the victim may be overwhelmed by hopelessness and loss. In each of these cases, the moment of death activates issues that can't be processed or resolved in that lifetime's moment of death, so a fragment of the self lingers around searching for resolution in a different lifetime.

I once had a client with physical and emotional issues that were concentrated across her shoulders. In trying to find the origin of this pattern, I found a past-life ghost lying across her shoulders. It was a remnant of a lifetime in which she had been the slave of a master who squeezed the life force out of her. She had become shriveled up like a raisin, barely kept alive, and in the deepest of depressions. It had been an especially sadistic exercise of power over her. It affected the client now by the influence of its deathly energy and depression. It cried out in her for some resolution, and it wanted attention. At the beginning of our healing session, the angels came in and led the work. The shriveled-up fragment stood up, straightened itself up, and grew into the shape of a full human being. As the integration began, the fragment was shown to contain soul essence, which revealed how very deeply this past life was affecting the client. Her past-life ghost and her light-body were rejoined through her soul matrix by the angels. It was a gradual process that eventually led to a full integration and a huge sense of relief for the client.

Healings like this are often a form of what is called 'soul retrieval' in shamanic traditions, because there appears to be 'lost' soul essence that needs to be retrieved and restored to the client. But in truth, your soul essence is always yours. It cannot be taken away from you, but you can participate in the illusion that you have lost soul essence, which is what my client had experienced in this traumatic life. And from her vantage point in that one lifetime, it was a perfectly reasonable conclusion given her pain and suffering. You can understand how often and how easily human beings are convinced of the illusion that something has been taken away from them, that they are spiritually injured or that they are somehow made powerless. Of course, events like these—having something taken away, becoming powerless—can actually happen in the physical world, so this gives support to the illusion that they also happen in the spiritual world—but only if a Creator Being participates in the illusion.

The 'Hungry Beast' and Denial

There is another phenomenon of dissociated consciousness very similar to the 'shadow' discussed earlier that I call the 'hungry beast.' The 'hungry beast' is a dissociated part of a person that must constantly be fed with negativity. Behind the beast is a need to maintain a state of depression and suffering, maybe as a coping mechanism to avoid facing a difficult truth or to avoid the challenge of changing one's life. For example, you might fear the challenge to accomplish something you want in your life, and instead you let yourself fail and feed negativity to the hungry beast. The 'beast' becomes like a spirit of depression that takes control of your life, because its entire purpose is to keep you feeding it.

A common element in many of these examples of dissociated consciousness is denial. At the core of the disassociation is something that must be kept away—something that emerges as a very deep wound that motivates the denial. There is always that key separation. Then on one side is the need to maintain the denial as part of outer self's reality, and on the other side is the wounded part that motivates the denial, but which stays isolated in its patterns of woundedness. The two can't communicate across the barrier of separation. This is more common than I think most people imagine. Bubbles of denial, even ones that project strength and power, always involve a wound.

The schism between competing patterns of consciousness often reveals themselves in the outer self through leaps of logic and behaviors that are disconnected from circumstances. From the denier's perspective, they have made a meaningful connection from point A to point B. But for someone carefully observing, point B has to do with something quite different from point A.

This kind of pattern doesn't necessarily have to involve leaps into negativity. I recognized this kind of schism once in a woman whose leaps of logic were often accompanied by bursts of enthusiasm. After she later became my client, I understood that her thoughts were jumping off track in a constant pattern of avoidance. A sunny point of view was a constant necessity for her outer self's denial. Whenever anyone pointed out shortcomings, she had an upbeat rejoinder to it. It was just that her responses were often unconnected to what triggered them. Something was constantly being avoided, and there seemed to be no way of penetrating her shield of optimism. And, of course, there was a dissociated part of herself that was vulnerable, afraid, and which needed lots of protection. These two aspects did not want to communicate with each other, and they simply resolved their predicament by co-existing. Two different reactions were going on at the same time: positive outward talk and inward terror. The client could not recognize this split, but she did acknowledge her periods of depression when she lacked the energy to maintain her shield. In our sessions it became clear that she feared a total collapse if her vulnerable side was ever revealed. Her dissociation was a coping mechanism that she had developed early in her life in response to her family's negativity. After some sessions focused on clearing the deep roots of her wounds, I believe that I really helped this client to have a better life, but the fundamental split was such a profound aspect of herself that she was not prepared to go any further during her time with me.

Bubbles of Separation

There are many different kinds of dissociated consciousness and many different levels at which it happens. Most people need some healing for their unintegrated child and their unresolved past lives. As probably seems obvious now, your consciousness dissociates because you have a reason. The reason can be very concrete and specific as it so often is with denial. Dissociated consciousness happens because you need for it to happen. You have created it in response to your own issues and contradictions. And all dissociated consciousness is contained within a bubble that holds the patterns and defines the boundaries around it. In this, you can see that bubbles are universal containers of separation. Dissociated consciousness requires a bubble to be maintained.

And you can also begin to see why it is important to heal dissociated patterns of consciousness. Your consciousness is continuously flowing through these bubbles, giving them energy. When you are giving energy to bubbles of illusion and separation, it is as if your consciousness is caught in traps. It is held back from rising to higher levels of unity and coherence. For example, you can never achieve what we call " when you are constantly feeding your dissociated consciousness. You are truly stuck in a separation that holds back your spiritual evolution.

What do you do then with your dissociated consciousness? These fragments only exist in these forms because something has caused them to be separated from the whole. In some cases, these fragments can be like passing dreams that are barely held together. Then again, they can be glued together so strongly by trauma and pain that they seem as unbreakable as a security safe. And at the same time, dissociated consciousness maybe teaches you an important lesson, because if you are capable of separating yourself in this way, then you must also be capable of un-separating yourself.

When you really understand how you have created dissociated consciousness, what about the opposite—reuniting consciousness? It is only a matter of changing your focus as

Creator Beings in order to heal your separations. The path of healing is about breaking bubbles—dissolving the separations including your dissociated consciousness. In your healing process, you break and make bubbles. With a bit more knowledge, you can become the architect and builder of a more harmonious state of consciousness.

HEALING PRACTICE: Integrating Dissociated Consciousness

Here again we extend the method of healing as a Creator Being and focus on integrating dissociated consciousness. We will focus on integrating the unintegrated child. This is probably the form of dissociated consciousness that most people can most easily recognize in themselves. But if you are aware of other forms of dissociated consciousness within yourself such as past lives, then this practice is easily adapted to those circumstances. In every case there is a bubble of a limited reality that helps to separate some part of your consciousness from the whole. It is important then in this process to transform the image you hold of the dissociated consciousness toward something whole, healthy, and fully integrated. This is also a process that bears repeating so that every aspect of the dissociation can be transformed by breaking its bubble.

1. Close your eyes, ask for a field of Divine Oneness, ask for the presence of your guides, and balance your auric field.
2. Think of yourself as the child at the time of the dissociation.
3. Close your eyes and visualize in front of you an image of yourself as that child. Visualize the specific circumstances of the dissociation. Let yourself experience its feelings, the pain and trauma, as fully as possible. Absorb yourself in the child's reality
4. Place your hands around that image of the dissociated child with palms facing inward.
5. Ask that an energy run between your hands that gives that child what it most needs and provides it with healing to be liberated, strong, and happy.
6. Continue the flow of healing energy while you guide the child's vision of their reality toward an alternative in which the events of the dissociation are experienced from a broader

perspective, maybe an adult perspective.

7. Continue the flow of healing energy until the feeling of dissociation is greatly reduced or becomes neutral.

8. When you are ready, relax your hands, open your eyes, and stay sensitive to how the work has affected you.

Chapter 12 — Understanding Bubbles

When a Creator Being creates a bubble, in most ways it is no different from any other creative act performed by a Creator Being. We have been examining bubbles now in a lot of different contexts. For example, there is a particularly simple type of bubble that we called a 'thought-form,' and there are progressively more complex forms of bubbles like 'contract bubbles' and 'narrative bubbles' leading up to very complex bubbles of 'dissociated consciousness.' All of these bubbles help us to make sense of our experience of the world. Bubbles turn out to be one of the most fundamental ways of organizing energy, and this helps us to understand how bubbles become a fundamental building block in the organization of our consciousness.

So, let's expand our discussion beyond looking at certain types. Up front, I want to avoid the common use of the term 'thought-form' as a general designation for all of these, because that term is too narrow to cover the huge variety of bubbles that exist. No, let's describe the characteristics of bubbles in the most open-ended and inclusive way possible. That is why we have adopted the very general name——'bubbles.' And this term is entirely befitting them because they have boundaries around them and a space on the inside just like an ordinary soap bubble. And while we might think of soap bubbles as totally inconsequential to our lives, these 'bubbles' are extremely important to understanding the way in which our consciousness works. Their space contains structures that guide our consciousness to flow along certain defined paths, and their boundaries define what is and isn't included within their influence. They are truly fundamental.

Those 'bubbles' that form around your head, what we have properly called 'thought-forms,' do provide us with a good working example. What they usually contain is the kind of thought patterns that you activate in everyday life. For example, they could contain a specific idea inside of them like: "I have to stop by the store" or "I can't do this kind of thing" or "My mother always treated me as if I were incompetent." These sorts of bubbles around the head are temporary and change from moment-to-moment. Your consciousness flows dynamically through the bubbles and follows along with their patterns because you created the patterns—the bubbles contain what you put into them. Often they are linked together in ways that create larger patterns of thinking with one bubble leading to another, sometimes in endless loops. The way that you sometimes experience your thoughts as jumping around from one thing to another or sometimes repeating the same idea over and over again is reflected in the way that your 'bubbles' are organized in groups around your head. Sometimes it seems that human beings can do hardly anything other than constantly creating lots and lots of these things!

These transitory bubbles around your head are the simplest form of something that manifests on a much larger plane of human activity. Essentially, bubbles are the result of a creative act that combines diverse things together to form a pattern. Whatever those things are—ideas, feelings, images, sensory information, etc.—they are bound together and interconnected. It is a very simple process. If you form a bubble primarily with mental energy, it is then largely mental. If you form it with emotional energy, then it is largely emotional. If it is formed with the energies of a complex behavior, then that is what it is. Making associations and forming patterns, these are fundamental to bubbles and to how human beings operate. Metaphorically, we could say that Creator Beings produce bubbles by blowing an intention into the field of potential creation, just like blowing soap bubbles—but this metaphor is pretty close to the actual truth.

Bubbles as Schemas

In order to take a closer look at 'bubbles,' we will borrow a term from cognitive psychology and make a connection between 'bubbles' and 'schemas.' In psychology, a 'schema' is a mental framework for an organized pattern of thought or behavior, typically a pattern that is used over and over again. That is almost exactly what we are talking about with 'bubbles.' From a cognitive perspective, schemas are patterns that lie in the brain, not neurological patterns *per se*, but functional models of how your mind works. And for us then, 'bubbles' could just as well be called 'psychic schemas' that hold just such a basic pattern for the flow of consciousness.

In its simplest form, a mental schema is a snapshot understanding that reduces the complexity of your experience to simple relationships. For example, in the early stages of life, the primal experience of encountering light leads to a mental schema for 'light.' We can imagine that this schema is initially based solely on repeated patterns of sensory experience—like seeing light. But as your experiences accumulate, the schema must expand to include concepts like how light emanates from a source. Maybe your schema for 'light' is augmented by its association with warmth, the sun, and maybe also how light divides space into illuminated and dark regions. Almost all of these aspects of light are shared experiences among all people. We all have a mental schema for 'light.' And that schema is also influenced by our shared psychic connections leading to 'psychic schemas' for 'light.' In the early stages of life, everyone is immersed in the psychic influence of others, and what 'light' means to us in term of its significance and expressiveness is shared psychically. You might call this a mythic understanding of 'light.'

Of course, your mental schema for 'light' must accommodate some degrees of divergence and individuality with the experience of light in different forms like distinctive light fixtures, indoor and outdoor lights, new light technologies, etc. And humanity is constantly seeking to harmonize its mental schemas and its psychic schemas around its understanding of 'light.' These mental schemas and psychic schemas are intertwined. This is a simple example, so simple that you hardly recognize that you think and experience in terms of simple schemas like 'light'—largely because your conscious mind is so preoccupied with managing your immediate problems moment-to-moment.

As another example, consider how the experience of being within a family leads to mental schemas and psychic schemas for 'family.' Such schemas must contain patterns for typical family members—mother, father, children—and they should explain the relationships of each to the others. And interestingly, humanity across the earth has been psychically working through adjustments to this psychic schema.' Such a change begins at the psychic level, and then it spreads next to the mental level. For example, a very prescriptive schema for 'family' has been deeply ingrained in many societies and incorporated within many individuals' sense of identity. But the evolving diversity of family groupings and family experiences that we recognize today has challenged humanity to form a new, more inclusive psychic schema for 'family.' The process of finding psychic resonance and commonality with each other is going on right now at psychic levels of communication, and slowly mental schemas are changing to match.

A very important aspect of the nature of your schemas is that they can contain links to your other schemas. This is a bit like having bubbles that contain other bubbles or that group together into clusters of bubbles. So, for example, once you establish a bubble for 'light,' which includes your ideas, feelings, and experiences about 'light,' it can be linked to your other bubbles that contain references to 'light.' For example, you could have a bubble, a psychic schema, for 'healing light' that includes a link to your original bubble for 'light' as well as other ideas, feelings, experiences, and connections related to healing. Of course, physical light and healing light are not the same thing. Physical light is taken in by your three-dimensional physical senses. Healing light is taken in by what we might call your psychic senses. Your psychic schemas for 'physical light' and 'healing light' will express those similarities and differences. Of course, healing light is not as easy to discuss or explain as physical light, so we are actually using 'light' as a metaphorical bridge between the two—we use your understanding of the physical sensation of light to make sense of a non-physical sensation. But, be on alert! In applying your psychic schema for 'healing light,' you might also carry over notions from physical light that are not relevant to 'healing light.' For example, physical light is blocked by the body, but you have to be clear that healing light penetrates it. This is one of the ways that your familiarity with the physical world can cause distortions in your psychic perception by taking words too literally!

Activating one psychic schema and then linking it to others is itself a creative act of association made by a Creator Being, and if these combine to form a pattern that is repeated, then this may lead to the creation of a bubble for a new psychic schema. In that way the number of bubbles proliferates and expands in a creative response to living. But for any one person, there tends to be only so many bubbles that can be activated and accessed at one time. This restriction provides a motivation to link many small bubbles together into larger bubbles that are easier to handle. For example, imagine how many bubbles you have linked together in making a bubble for 'television.' The extent to which bubbles can be interconnected with one to another is almost infinite. The combinations naturally form large networks of bubbles that are linked together. These networks are built up at many different levels—some are simple and local, and some link together huge groups of schemas about how the world works.

Complex networks of bubbles can constitute a shared worldview, a legacy of how to make sense of the human experience. Their combinations define our cultures, sub-cultures, and so on. And so it is with the psychic realities of nations, subgroups within the society, families, etc.—their worldview is sustained by shared bubbles. Creator Beings create in response to the challenges that they experience, and their creations are often part of a shared effort to organize and make sense of their experience. Whenever humanity needs to codify its understanding, then the creativity of Creator Beings manifests to produce schemas that provide explanations. This is true both of the mental schemas that are manifested in the brain, as well as the psychic schemas that are manifested as bubbles. Human beings simply create bubbles as a normal and necessary part of living.

Chapter 13 — Collective Consciousness

The way it happened, I once had a client who called me in an emergency. She said that she was being attacked by negative energy. In particular she believed that a former lover who was some kind of dark magician was using his skills to send her this negative energy. Along with this, she thought that she had been invaded by dark entities. She needed me to clear her light-body so that she could finally relax and sleep better, because all of this was keeping her awake at night and affecting her ability to work. And when she arrived for her session, there was indeed a lot of dark energy to clear away. Then she wanted me to confirm that her former lover was the one sending this negativity to her—but I couldn't really say that. I chose instead to turn her attention toward how to stop all of this from happening. I asked her if we could work on why she was attracting this negativity and why she couldn't protect herself. I said that there had to be underlying reasons on her side. That opened the door to some additional sessions.

I learned during our subsequent meetings that my client had grown up in a rural family that was immersed in a rather severe version of Christianity that put a great deal of emphasis on sin and punishment. Her family had continually reinforced to her how very important it was for the family to stick together and to hold strong to their faith. And to me, this was a pattern that had been passed down as part of her family's legacy since the days long ago when her ancestors were pioneers working to tame the wilderness. Having fought to survive, past generations had depended on the family members staying together and serving the family's collective needs. Their kind of religion had served the purpose of supporting this family imperative.

My client had long ago moved away to a city where she found employment in the financial sector. Anyone would have said that she was very successful in her life, even if she was a little over-stressed. She had also found her way into a more congenial and uplifting church, one that provided a very different setting for religion in her life. By this she had successfully transformed the influences of her early life into something that better reflected her own identity, which came across as very sweet and accommodating. She was trying hard not to be pulled back into the emotional despair she experienced as a child. She continued contact with her family, even though she disliked being with them, and visits often triggered feelings of depression. In truth, in spite of all the changes in her life, this client gave the impression on the surface of someone who was very passive. Her relationship with the lover she described to me happened totally at his initiation. The relationship only ended when he moved away, and she had not started any relationships since.

After each of our sessions, the client reported that the attacks of negative energy had disappeared and that she could get some normal sleep, but after some days she would contact me to say that the negative energy was back again. She continued to see me for some number of sessions, and we worked intensively to clear negativity and to build up her light-body's natural protections. It was hard work for her, but we began to examine and cancel many negative beliefs that she held about herself and especially negative beliefs about her relationship with God. And while she had seemingly moved on in terms of her own religion, she had not really let go of some core beliefs she acquired as a child, most of which were based on the understandings of a child's mind and were therefore difficult for her to access and deal with as a mature adult. She covered up her negative feelings with symbols and artifacts of positive ones like the little angels she wore all of the time. In truth, underneath of her sweet appearance she had buried a belief that she was a terrible person and that God had condemned her just as her family taught her. She had never really freed herself of her family's belief system.

I could see that she had also taken into her light-body numerous echoes of the consciousness of her family members. To my sight these were like phantom images of her family members that were present in her field and almost speaking to her and telling her their condemning opinions about what she did. And in this too, these presences in her light-body reflected a child's perception and understanding—the images were clearly her own simple portraits of her family members as seen through the eyes of a child. You could say that her thoughts were not her own, but a constant argument that was going on within her between herself and the family whose approval she would never receive.

As we progressed in our sessions, we hit some major obstacles. One obstacle was the anger that she felt toward her family and which at the same time she totally denied. To me it was full onset rage. That anger spilled over toward her colleagues at work, and toward certain social groups, especially toward 'lazy people' like immigrants. Despite my efforts, she was honestly not ready to let go of this anger—period. I understood that in truth she wanted love and acceptance from her family, but letting go of the anger would threaten her whole identity that was constructed in reaction to her family. That was the 'solution' she had worked out for herself. She was left with the wall of judgment and disapproval that had existed between herself and her family. Even her apparent passivity was a coping mechanism that allowed her to survive her family's judgments by just going along with things.

This client had created a sense of self that responded to her life's situation and resolved many issues, but now the biggest obstacle to moving ahead was the client's inability to assume some level of responsibility for her situation. She was in total denial that anything she held inside of herself was causing her problems. After all, she was a good person living according to her notions of what it means to be a good person. She worked hard at being a good person, in spite of the fact that this good person was being victimized by others. Her focus was completely on her outer self. I thought that the condemnation that she held within herself was redirected to others on the outside. This was a powerful demonstration of the power of denial.

We never completely stopped the negative energy from coming to her. To me, she was clearly the one sending it to herself. Her shadow was ruling her inner life and attacking the outer life that fought to ignore it. After a while, she stopped coming to me. I learned later that she had found another healer to work with. It was a disappointment to me that I hadn't helped her any more significantly than I did, but, of course, I accept that I am not always the healer that people need at a particular moment.

But after this was all over, I was asking myself why her issues were so intractable. The answer that eventually came to me was that none of the issues we had worked on were totally personal to my client. I had been clearing her light-body, but the issues themselves were not about her *per se*. If I looked at her situation from a broader perspective, I saw that her issues were shared with many of the people around her. The power of the issues that held her in check was collective. Nothing was totally individual. She was totally submerged in collective bubbles, and they ruled her life. Her family's legacy issues of staying bound together were collective. Her family's punitive form of Christianity was collective. The powerful psychological mechanism of her punishing herself as a bad person was shared with many others and collective. And her pattern of blaming others for the failures of her life was collective. She had tried to escape from the harsh emotional environment of her family, but in truth she had simply re-implemented the family's controlling bubbles in new forms.

I had been working to liberate my client from dysfunctional patterns, but she wasn't working to liberate herself. That wasn't her goal. Her identity had been established in her early life within a context established by her collective bubbles, and when she grew into an adult, she had carried that context into the world she now inhabited. She didn't want to escape the web of her collective bubbles; she just wanted it to work better for her. I hadn't quite seen the forest for the collective bubbles.

After that insight, I realized that the influence of the collective was similar with all of my clients. There was almost nothing in my healings that was truly individual. The power behind what we imagine to be our own personal issues is almost always collective. The extent to which we see these things as individual—individual to ourselves and about us personally—is a trick of perspective. In the flow of day-to-day life, that influence is often hidden from our eyes—also a part of the unexpressed. Early in life we simply accept the collective bubbles that are around us—family bubbles, peer group bubbles, community bubbles, societal bubbles—and we inherit all of their collective limitations and dysfunctional patterns.

Collective Bubbles

An understanding of bubbles is important to making sense of the relationship between the individual and the collective. We are each connected to collective bubbles just as if they were our own individual bubbles. If you could see your total network of bubbles, it would reveal how deeply embedded in the collective you are. There are bubbles that hold your everyday patterns of thinking, bubbles that hold your shared values and experiences, and even bubbles that contain your whole beliefs systems—especially societal belief systems, because these bubbles are held in common with all of the people who are around you. It seems that there are bubbles at all levels of human organization—the individual, the family, the tribe, the community, the society as a whole, etc. In truth, you are embedded in multiple collectives at all these different levels, and your collective bubbles are shared with people from a handful to millions.

How is it that we share so many bubbles? Take a moment to visualize this: Out in the great psychic sea there is a place where all of our bubbles are clustered together. In that place everyone can be linked to the bubbles and access them as if they were their own. So, in early life when we are creating our personal reality, we are connecting to the collective bubbles that are already around us and floating in the psychic sea. Creating our sense of self is essentially an act of co-creation.

Each person who holds a connection to a bubble is giving energy to that bubble, adding to its power, and making it more easily available to others. Even bubbles shared by a few people in a family can become very powerful if enough energy is given to them. For example, there are some families who become deeply entrenched in bubbles of denial. A recurrent situation is one in which something is wrong with one of the parents— alcoholism, mental illness, narcissism, etc. The facts may be obvious, but the need for a bubble that maintains the appearance of normalcy is so strong that it overpowers the family and drives them into a deeper and deeper dysfunction that seems impossible to change. So, you can imagine the strength of bubbles empowered by large groups of people.

Some of our collective bubbles become quite massive and extremely powerful. They have virtually forced their reality on you, even if you think of them as commonplace and ordinary. Take a familiar example: you might say that the medical concept of 'illness' is a large bubble shared by most of western society. It is constructed out of many smaller bubbles that explain exactly how illness and medical treatment work. Such bubbles can take on a level of strength that overwhelms an individual who cannot possibly see any reality that lies outside this bubble. The bubble gains its enormous power from the many, many people who join in and give energy to it.

At the same time, by virtue of how the energy of unfolding creation is constantly pushing evolution forward, none of these collective bubbles are actually permanent. Some collective bubbles are like fads that pass quickly because there is so little on-going energy to sustain them. Others are continually fed energy through repeated reinforcement by many people; they take on increasing strength, and they endure for much longer periods of time. The power of the collective to sustain its bubbles is made obvious by how hard it is to change them. A bubble can take on the appearance of absolute truth simply as a reflection of the power given to it by a collection of people. 'The earth is flat' seemed to be an absolute truth until the collective had reason to shift to a new truth. It wasn't just an idea; it was a special reality contained in a bubble that shaped how people perceived the world. They couldn't see the curvature of the earth that was right in front of them. The belief lasted for centuries, but change it did. So, no matter how solid the bubble appears, it will not persist without reinforcement.

Collective bubbles are the foundation of humanity's collective consciousness, but often when people use that term 'collective consciousness,' they are referring only to a particular level of cultural consciousness. With only slight reflection we can understand that 'collective consciousness' is a natural co-creation of any group of people, large or small, because all groups are joined through psychic communication that is supported by their collective bubbles. Then too, collective bubbles are part of how our shared human legacy is passed on from one generation to the next. Each person born into life on earth finds themselves swimming in the psychic sea filled with the collective bubbles that humanity has co-created over the centuries. This too is part of our collective consciousness. The network of bubbles passed on and sustained from one generation to the next surrounds the earth and holds the framework in which human consciousness operates. You might say that our collective consciousness exists in a zone between the finite world of everyday life and the infinite expanse of the psychic sea.

Healing ourselves as a path to liberating ourselves has to acknowledge the presence and the power of collective bubbles. You are embedded in collective bubbles at all levels of social organization, and these collective bubbles provide a context around your individual issues. Sometimes they are the trigger that actually creates your issues. Clearly, collective bubbles are necessary to the functioning of a society, and at the same time, some collective bubbles, like bubbles of collective denial, are damaging to you and to everyone.

The question is: How do you manage your relationship to the collective, while attempting to heal yourself? Part of the answer comes in grasping how much of your power you have given away, not just to the individuals in your life, but to the collective. If you could see it clearly, you would realize how deeply interdependent everyone is on the collective to give them what they need—to give them the basics of life, and to give them the psychic energy they need to build their lives. After all, we are very tribal animals and our interdependence is reflected at the physical level of our lives and at the psychic level. This reveals an almost invisible level at which we give our power away, that is, to the collective at the psychic level. So many of our unexamined collective bubbles are disempowering to us.

Being so deeply embedded in the collective, we don't realize how different our interrelationship with the collective could be if we looked to ourselves for what we need at the psychic level. That is the reason behind the exercises that I do with my clients in which they give themselves whatever energy they most need. The idea is that they shift the source of the psychic energy they need to themselves. The impact of this exercise is often reflected in their level of shock—the notion of giving power to themselves never occurred to them before. They may have looked everywhere for help, but not to themselves! Through this exercise, you learn that you, only you, are true the source of your own light. And this becomes an important part of maintaining your sovereignty, as described by Amorah Quan Yin earlier in the book. Being your own sovereign ultimately leads you to being the source of your own energy, without giving it away to the collective.

This is our evolutionary process, both for you as an individual and for humanity as a whole. Step-by-step you must take back your power and break free from those collective bubbles that restrict your progress toward Oneness. The work that you do individually by breaking free is also essential to humanity's evolution, because your personal issues are almost always spring from collective issues in disguise. By withdrawing your power from collective bubbles that restrict your spiritual progress, you also help humanity to withdraw its power from bubbles that restrict its progress. It is especially important for each of us to break the restrictive bubbles that were woven into the fabric of our early life. We all grow up in a web of collective bubbles that are essentially invisible to us, and we all find ourselves struggling against what seems like invisible barriers. These kinds of collective bubbles are a kind of blind spot in humanity's vision of itself, because the restrictions that they hold are seemingly invisible. In this, there is so much that we can do together to bring the invisible into view.

And we must give power to the collective bubbles that promote our harmony with Oneness. Humanity's collective consciousness includes many bubbles that support our wellbeing and harmony; maybe we just have to work a little harder to find them and empower them in our lives. We can shift the balance of our power from the restrictive to the supportive. And we must create new collective bubbles that advance our spiritual evolution. As Creator Beings we hold the vision of the collective consciousness we want to create for ourselves and for humanity.

Chapter 14 — A New Client, Part III

Ella is coming for another session today. A summer and an autumn have passed since we started our sessions together. During that time Ella has worked hard and approached her healing process with an ever-growing commitment. She is re-inventing herself, and she feels more and more in control. She has also started the class in light-body healing that my wife Ulla teaches. It is called 'Divine Oneness.' There Ella has found a connection to a small community of people who share her commitment to changing the orientation of their lives. You can feel that there is this intangible something that draws such people together. They may have such different life histories— they are young and they are old—but they all believe that they are improving their lives and liberating themselves from something that has invisibly held them back. Ella may not believe that being a healer is part of her future, but she has found herself on a path to something that she knows she wants.

This has also been a period during which I have sought greater understanding of the collective consciousness and how to liberate my clients from the power of the collective issues that hold them back—to move beyond personal healing to breaking free of collective bubbles. I have been thinking about changes in my usual techniques and procedures—but in the end I haven't really changed very much, at least nothing that could be observed from the outside. But inwardly as I understand and experience things, I have changed a lot.

Right from the start of the session, I know that I think about setting space differently. I think now about how the space that I set can have an effect on my client's bubbles. I have always tried to create a space that had a high frequency, but I understand its effect differently now because I am thinking about how limiting bubbles can be dissolved during the healing session. For example, the space that I create around the client must be a bubble that is more open and expansive than those that the client needs to release. Setting space means building a bubble of an alternative reality in which the client's issues can be dissolved and in which the client can evolve.

I think that I have come to know Ella quite well by now. When I do my preparations for our session, I know what it is that she has been thinking about for herself. Step-by-step she has been building a new image of herself as a free and vibrant person. She is discovering how to be her authentic self. It is as if she is throwing away some old clothes and taking on to some new clothes that fit her better. She has embraced the process of manifesting that new vision of herself, but it is not the only vision that influences her. There is still the lingering vision of herself as a failure and as screw-up, even though it has less and less to do with her life in the present.

She changed jobs a few months ago. The last time I saw her she was still finding out what this new job would be like for her. But she assures me that it is less stressful than her last job and that the people are less nasty to each other. It feels that way to me too. Some company's internal cultures are quite abusive to people, but her new company is not like that. From what I sense, it is truly more service-oriented, and therefore sensitivity to people is important. Ella has not established a new relationship with a man at this time. She told me that she was open but didn't quite trust herself yet. I think that given what her relationship with her parents was like, Ella's internal male and female sides still have not found peace with each other.

Ella did send me an email a few days ago with some priorities for this healing. First, to continue work on her self-confidence, and second, to help her to attract the right kind of relationship to herself.

It is easy meeting her now. We can move right away to the healing space and take our places. We begin.

G: "Thank you for your email. That really helps me to prepare for our session. Is there anything else that you want to catch me up on before we start?"

E: "No. The only other thing I might mention is that I had a conversation with my parents. It was maybe the easiest that I have had in a long time, because I realized that I didn't feel bad afterwards."

G; "Ok, can you describe how you did feel?"

E: "Yeah, I felt kind of calm and even, like it was completely normal. I think it is the first time that my buttons didn't get pushed by something that they said, not even my dad."

G: "Do you think that your relationship with them is different now?"

E: "Yeah, I am a bit weary. Cautious, I guess. My mom is always ok with me. She tiptoes around. I am still a bit on guard that my dad will go off about something."

G: "Seems that you are really holding your space with them."

E: "Yeah, I didn't collapse right away. I didn't collapse at all."

G: "Great, you have really come a long way in your relationship with them."

Ella and I go through the process of setting space for our session. I am very much aware that Ella really commits herself to this as she settles in.

G: "Ella, the first thing I would like you to do is a visualization. I would like you to visualize in front of you an image of yourself as you truly are right now—you as you are now at this stage in your life. Be honest and true to yourself."

Ella sits quietly and focuses.

G: "When you are ready, I would like you to put your hands around this image, one on each side, palms facing inward."

I wait while Ella prepares herself and then puts her hands around the image she is holding.

G: "Now I want you to run energy through your hands and to give yourself whatever it is that you need to become stronger and healthier as a person, whatever you need to become the best you can possibly be."

While Ella is working in this way—giving herself what she needs—I am looking at what appears to me to be a cluster of complex energy sitting on her right shoulder. It is all tied up with her belief in her failures and her feelings of self-hatred. For Ella, this seems all personal, but to me it is essentially a bubble that maintains the truth of her parents' viewpoint that Ella a 'screwed-up' who can't manage her life. Their attitude is part of a collective bubble of distrust between two generations who have grown up in very different realities. As I hold this bubble, I shift my perception to a space outside of this bubble. This bubble needs to be broken and replaced with another one, one in which all of these issues are transformed into passages of maturity.

G: "Ella, I would like you to include an image of your parents in the visualization you are holding. When you are ready, tell me how they look."

E: "This is hard. It doesn't work too well. They seem really out of place."

G: "What do you think their reaction is to being here with you."

E: "No, they don't fit here with me. They want to get away off to themselves. They are not ready for this."

G: "Good. Just let them go."

This is perfect. Ella is creating her own vision of herself, and importantly by standing outside of the bubble of her parents' vision, she has broken the power of the old bubble.

Ella and I have both worked for a while now. I want to shift focus to her issue about relationships. There is a lot of pain here from the relationship she recently left, but there is also the fear of a breakdown in male and female roles that she took on from her parents. As long as that remains in place, I think that she will likely recreate that broken male-female relationship in her own life.

G: "Ella, that is going very well. How does the image of yourself look now?"

E: "I think that I look stronger. And yeah, I think that I don't look as young as before. I don't mean that I look old, but I my image changed."

G: "That is really beautiful. You certainly do have a lot more strength and self-awareness to draw on now in shaping your path in life."

I am sensing something that I didn't quite anticipate. When I said that, I felt a pull of sadness and longing in Ella's heart. I see a ball of dark energy uncovered there like a wound deep inside of her capacity to feel and to love. The wound is now open for healing. I am thinking that Ella's Higher Self has guided her to this moment.

G: "How are you feeling right now?"

E: "Sorry, I kind of drifted away there."

G: "Are you aware of anything going through your mind?"

E: "Yeah, I was thinking, 'What's the use.' What if this is leading me nowhere? Nothing has really changed."

G: "You just brought up something that is a deep issue for you. Are there other times when you feel this way?"

E: "Oh yeah. I just went back to how I felt in high school when I started to give up. Because there was no use in doing anything. Everything was a mess."

G: "That feeling is still with you. I was actually asking about more recently. Have you felt that way more recently?

E: "I think mostly at night. I think that I get depressed before going to bed."

G: "Would you like to work to get rid of that?"

E: "I feel so sad like I am just trapped."

There is a wave of desperate feeling that I read as a cry for help. She must have felt this many times in her teens when no one answered her call for help. And right now it came up when letting go of her parents' beliefs about her. And in my vision, she has attracted a group of healing spirits to her. They form a circle around her. I don't want her to get into defensive thoughts. I need to have her shift her perspective.

G: "Ella, there are helping spirits who have come now to help you heal yourself. Do you accept their help?"

E: "Yes.

She is holding out her arms in a gesture of receiving.

G: "We are going to do some work on your heart chakra to remove the pain that is held there. Are you ready for that?"

E: "You bet.

Back when I first began to learn about the light-body, I thought of the chakras as separate parts of the energetic system. I think that all of my teachers understood how interconnected the light-body is, but I think that every pedagogy has to simplify in order to guide the students safely through their first steps. That is how you learn to see the details: maybe most people need to learn to see energetic structures before they can experience the whole. I realize now that my early understanding of the light-body was itself a bubble of understanding created and supported by many teachers working hard to create clear models of the energy system that could be communicated to others. Some of these people were inspired by medical models of healing and by an admiration of specialized knowledge. Others were inspired by the teachings of indigenous people with their continuity of knowledge going back to ancient times. In truth, there are multiple models of healing that are mixing and transforming in today's world. I think that we will eventually evolve a truly contemporary understanding of healing the light-body that has blended many influences. And as our contemporary spiritual consciousness changes, so will our fundamental assumptions about healing.

An important practical lesson that I have come to realize is that I am always present in the healing. I know that at some point most every healer is taught about the importance of being detached and absolutely neutral in their healing sessions. You strive to be a 'pure channel' for the healing energies, and you certainly must avoid triggering your own issues during the healing session. After years of thinking exactly the same way, what I want to say now is a recognition of something that it more fundamental. Even after mastering detachment, the healer's energy is always engaged in the healing process. There is no separation. I am the client and I am myself. I join the bubble that needs healing, and I shift to the space outside the bubble that holds a higher frequency. My detachment holds a power to disentangle energies that are tied up in blockages and traumas. It is a natural part of the healing transaction: I bring everything that I am to the process.

Something has certainly happened to me. I can't approach systems as separate anymore. I think that in any one person's chakra is a universe that is connected to all. There is no separation. I bring myself to the process and the process happens. What is transformed is transformed. What I know is that my participation has an effect. And my ability to move consciously in and out of bubbles influences what happens.

The healing spirits and I are in the space of Ella's heart chakra. Her pain is dark and intense, and that reflects the level of Ella's emotional sensitivity. Things went so badly for her early in her life. Her pain is contained in a bubble of a limited reality, and within this bubble, Ella is trapped in her parents' negativity toward her. I experience the reality that the bubble holds. At the same time the guides and I stay in a place of loving neutrality. The bubble that holds the pain is broken when viewed from the perspective of greater acceptance and love.

G: "Tell me about when your father hit you."

E: "Yeah, he was out of control. He must have been drinking. I was so afraid of him, and then I walked right into it. I guess I knew that it was coming. You know, I used to think that I deserved it. Now, that is crazy, isn't it?"

Ella has tears in her eyes.

G: "And where was your mom?"

E: "She was there and just helpless. She was no use."

G: "How do you feel?"

E: "I feel really angry at them. What a terrible situation. What fuck-ups they were. Boy, look at the irony in that!"

It has maybe taken a few minutes. I work to dissolve what is left of the pain. The bubble is broken. It can't sustain itself in the same way anymore. It feels more and more like a phantom of the past.

G: "And how do you feel?"

E: "Something happened. I feel better now."

I wait until things have settled down.

G: "Ok, lets work on something else. Maybe we do some work on attracting a better relationship into your life. Do you think we can do another visualization? This is similar to something we have done before. I would like you to visualize your female aspect and your male aspect separately, one to the left and one to the right. Do you remember? Is this comfortable for you?"

E: "Yes, I remember working on my male and female sides before like this."

G: "This will be a little different this time. Tell me when you have those two aspects clearly visualized."

After a pause,

E: "Yeah, I feel ready."

G: "Ok, I want you to ask your male aspect to look at the female aspect, and then to tell you what the male aspect sees."

I think that Ella has drawn her strength mostly from her male side. We know that it was the relationship with her father that she favored earlier in her life. To me, she has never fully stepped into her female side. She has been submissive in her relationships, but what I am hoping to draw out is strength in her feminine.

After a few moments, Ella speaks.

E: "Yeah, he says that the female aspect is weak and unreliable. She is very incomplete as a woman. He doesn't have much respect for her."

"Wow," I am thinking to myself.

G: "Maybe she needs help in coming forth. Please put your hands around the image you have of her and give her what she needs to come out of her shell."

E: "She is so collapsed. I think that I don't really know her. How did it come to this?"

Ella has become a bit tearful again and needs to wipe her eyes while she is running the energy through her hands. I am also running energy to assist Ella in her process.

After some moments,

G: "How is she looking now?"

E: "She is beginning to stand up. She has pushed back her hair, and she is finding her strength. I think that she really needs love."

G: "Lets focus on sending her love and acceptance."

We continue for some minutes.

G: "And now?"

E: "She has really changed. Receiving love made such a difference to her."

G: "Tell me when you are ready to move on."

E: "Yeah, yeah. I am ready."

G: "Now, pull back to a place where you can see both your female and male aspects again. When you are ready, ask your female aspect to tell you what she sees in looking at the male."

E: "What she sees is a crippled man. He is wounded and this makes him full of anger. His anger is a kind of defense against the world. But he is also hates himself."

G: "Put your hands around his image and give to him the healing that he needs."

E: "It is not so easy. There is so much anger."

G: "Lets focus on the anger then. Ask to see the anger that he is holding back."

E: "There is so much anger. Anger that life has turned out so badly."

G: "I don't know if you have started using crystalline energy in the healing class, but right now I would like you to ask for a connection to the crystalline grid of the earth. Can you do that?"

E: "Yeah, I did this once before."

G: "I want you to run the crystalline energy between your hands and through the image of your male side. Use this energy to dissolve the structure behind the anger."

Some time passes as Ella works on this. Meanwhile I am assisting. Ella needs balance between her male and female sides. She needs a healthy male side to bring better governance into her life. Without that balance, her female side will be lacking complete power in the feminine. The ideal that I aim for is a balance between the sacred masculine and the sacred feminine.

G: "How is it going?"

E: "Yeah, the anger seems less powerful now."

G: "What does he need now?"

E: "He wants to regain his composure. He stands up and straightens himself. He tries to fix his clothes. He could be so much more, but he really doesn't know what to do."

G: "Maybe you could shift now to giving him what he needs in order to heal himself."

I am thinking ahead to my next session with Ella in which we may be able to bring these two aspects closer together—closer to balance and integration.

E: "This is good. It feels as if something has filled a hole inside of me, but I feel kind-a empty too."

G: "You are in a transition. In the meantime, let's put a Field of Healing and Integration around you. You remember that one?"

E: Yeah, no problem. I use that a lot at night, especially when I feel depressed."

G: "We ask for a Field of Healing and Integration to be placed around you and to be held in place through this day."

Ella takes a deep breath

G: You should be sure to ask for it again tonight and the next several nights."

E: "Yeah, ok."

G: "How do you feel?"

E: "Yeah, ok. I feel kind of half here."

G: "Remember the exercise of gathering all of your points of awareness in your pineal? Can you do that now?"

E: "Right. I call on all of my points of awareness to return to me from wherever they are. I call them to gather in my pineal."

I give her a minute to discover where all of her points of awareness have been.

G: "How is it going?"

E: "Some of my awareness was back with my parents."

G: "Just take the time to bring all of your awareness here and now."

I can see that Ella has become more present.

G: "We just did some pretty intensive work. Do you have any questions?"

E: "Yeah, the question I have is what advice do the guides have for me?"

G: "Can you be more specific?"

E: "I mean that I am open to whatever the guides tell me I should do to make my life better."

I am thinking that this question is a regression back into her more passive female aspect. It is not unusual in my experience that old patterns try to reassert themselves immediately after a major shift.

G: "Hmm. I guess that what I want to say is that you have reached a stage at which your decisions are far less controlled by your old habits and compulsions. That might feel as if you are missing something that you used to rely on. The guides are happy to give assistance to you, but you are shaping your own life now."

E: "Whoa, wait a second. You mean that the guides are abandoning me just as I am really making some progress?"

Here is another old pattern trying to reemerge—that pattern of feeling abandoned by her parents, only it has been transferred in this moment to "the guides."

G: "No, I am only affirming what has been true all along. It was true when you were a small child. It was true when you were a teen. You are the author of your own life. The guides will not and cannot take that power away from you. Maybe it will take some getting used to."

E: "Geez. Ok, I get it."

G: "The true messengers of the light don't want to control you or tell you what is right or wrong. You are closer and closer to experiencing real freedom. You are your own master."

E: "That is tough love."

G: "Yeah. That is well said."

We close the session in the usual way.

Chapter 15 — Creating Everyday Reality

The story of bubbles so far: we have approached the 'bubble' as a broad concept that represents how we create areas of separation between ourselves and Oneness. For example, the limitations and blockages that we create in our light-bodies are held within bubbles. Dissociated consciousness is held within bubbles. In a broad sense, bubbles contain whatever Creator Beings put into them. And much of the time, what we Creator Beings put into them are our ordinary, repeated patterns of thought and behavior that are just like mental schemas. Some kinds of bubbles are individual, while most are collective. What we put into our collective bubbles becomes the basis of our shared reality. It is these patterns that provide most of our framework for everyday life.

So, in a very important sense, bubbles can be viewed as a form of knowledge. They describe the interrelationship among some number of things that form a pattern, any kind of pattern, and they do it in a very flexible way. Our vast network of collective bubbles is like a library holding humanity's shared knowledge. We all have access to this library because we joined the library psychically at a very early age—in fact, maybe even as early as when we first arrived on Earth! Accessing these bubbles is a normal, everyday psychic phenomenon. It is really so obvious and so immediate that no one notices it—because we are all inside of the everyday reality created by our collective bubbles. And in our everyday life, we tend to access the same bubbles over and over, day after day. It is as if we check out the same books from the library over and over.

Your experience of the everyday world is determined by your network of bubbles. You need these bubbles in order to make any sense of the world around you. Or, turn that around and say: the bubbles ARE the sense that you make of the world around you. You must intuitively know that without the clarity that these bubbles provide, the world around you would just seem like noise—as Shakespeare says "sound and fury signifying nothing." Without your bubbles, nothing would have any significance, and you would have no patterns of behavior to fall back on. And so, you like everyone else hold onto your bubbles quite tenaciously.

The bubbles are also the way in which you attribute meaning to your personal reality. So bear with me in this metaphor: you might say that the bubbles are like the furniture with which you decorate the interior of your house—only instead of your house you are decorating the inner space of your life. And even though it is a personal reality that you are creating, most of these bubbles are collective. Like the furniture with which you decorate your personal room, the bubbles of your inner space are almost entirely acquired from the warehouse of the collective. You make choices from within the network of collective bubbles, and you fashion a space for yourself that reflects your individuality. From that perspective you can understand that the inner space of your life often has more in common with other people than you might ordinarily think!

The Collective As Personal

As you may realize by now, even when your limitations and dysfunctional patterns appear to be unique to your personal circumstances, the concepts and the background behind these limitations and patterns are almost always products of collective bubbles. Something as fundamental as a lack of self-worth requires the supporting collective belief that people do have different levels of worth. Is such a belief obvious or necessary? Certainly not, but it is a product of cultural perspectives that see people through a lens that is economic or prejudicial or whatever.

As another example, consider how many people experience shame—most commonly caused by their parents early in life, often in response to some behavior that is quite typical in childhood. It might have been something as trivial as accidentally breaking something or coming home with dirty clothes. In any case, lots of parents not only correct the mistake, they also provoke a feeling of shame. What compels them to do this? They undoubtedly were drawn into the collective bubble of shame when they were children.

Almost everyone experiences their shame as intensely personal, but behind the personal shame is a collective belief that shame is appropriate or necessary in shaping behavior. The potential to feel shame appears to be part of our biological legacy, that is, shame is a behavioral pattern that is hard-wired into human neurobiology. We all are programmed to feel shame and to try to avoid it. But as with many human behaviors, we can easily become overly fixated and creative with embellishing shame, and then connecting it to more and more aspects of our lives. We all probably know an adult who has been raised by shaming parents and for whom shame is a constant companion. This is a product of living within a collective bubble of cultural dysfunction—a subculture in which the fear of shame is like an open wound.

When you connect to collective bubbles like shame, you also give energy to them. The more energy they receive from you, the stronger and more persistent they are. It is in this way that the bubbles you access over and over again in everyday life can come to dominate your life and the lives of others. It is a kind of feedback system. So for example, giving your energy to everyday tasks with little meaning means that you reinforce having little meaning in your life. As another example, if you give sufficient energy to dysfunctional patterns like low self-worth or shame, then these patterns can become so strong that they appear inescapable. It shouldn't be surprising how often we feed energy to the very bubbles that keep us trapped in dysfunction. Once you are inside the bubbles, it becomes more and more difficult to see anything outside the bubbles. You see nothing but your lack of self-worth or your shame. It is rather like a pattern of denial. Effectively, you deny the possibility that you are worthy or that you have nothing to be ashamed of.

As must also be obvious now, it is not just hard-won truth that is held in our collective bubbles. Most of our personal issues are the direct result of our collective misperceptions and misjudgments. Our illusions and misunderstandings are shared—our coping mechanisms and denials too—some conscious and some unconscious. Yes, humanity as a whole can make some really big mistakes! And in particular, individual societies and subgroups can become absolutely driven in the pursuit of total misconceptions enshrined like absolute truth within their collective bubbles—bubbles of denial, bubbles of desperation, etc. Maybe you could say that every single war gives evidence to this.

Bubbles of the Past Events

When a group of Creator Beings share an experience, their perceptions of that experience may fuse together in a collective bubble, and that bubble becomes the group's collective reference point for their shared experience. If this experience was particularly intense or if it didn't harmonize with the group's collective beliefs, then this bubble may stand out from other experiences that are more easily assimilated and seemingly forgotten. Such a bubble with unresolved aspects can exert a powerful influence on the group, which could be trying to reach a resolution with the event long after it is over. Consider the 9/11 attack on the New York World Trade Center. The images are still quite vivid in people's minds, and many things are deeply unresolved about this event. The 9/11 bubble, as well as its many supporting bubbles, will stay in the collective consciousness for a long time. We can call this kind of bubble an 'event bubble.' And even though catastrophes from the distant past are more difficult to recall, event bubbles from long ago can still influence us today. For example, humanity still holds the ancient fall of Atlantis in their collective consciousness, and it has created a psychic resonance with subsequent catastrophes in human history.

We have said before that bubbles often provide a simplified view of something more complex. Real events can have lots of details, and, in truth, most of these details can be quite beside the point. Event bubbles provide a simplified viewpoint that makes sense of the event for us, and generally they tell us how we feel about the event. Whether these are global events like 9/11 or personal events like the breakup of a relationship, our sense of those events is captured in a bubble that simplifies the event and provides us with a particular viewpoint and a particular feeling about what took place.

Interestingly, a great deal of your everyday, on-going experience is shaped by the event bubbles of your past, especially your unresolved past. You may be alive and conscious in the present, but it is as if your light-body carries around all of your unresolved loose ends while you are still trying to figure things out. Human societies maintain their collective histories in books and stories that tell us which events are important and how we are supposed to think about them. This kind of 'past' is essentially a collection of event bubbles.

As an individual, you often hold onto a personal narrative about your life that is just like those books, a narrative that tries to explain your personal history, your ups and downs and changes, and all of this is a collection of event bubbles. For many people, this personal narrative that they have created keeps them trapped in old patterns. For example, a narrative that tells you that you were ok until you got off track in high school or that you were broken down by a bad marriage, such a narrative can acquire so much energy that it becomes a theme that takes over your life. It imposes its particular significance onto new events simply because you are holding onto it so tightly. This personal narrative, that you take to be an absolute reality, is based on a collection of event bubbles that have created that meaning for you.

You should ask yourself: what is the actual meaning of the 'past' to you now living in the present? If, in essence, your past is a collection of event bubbles that you have assembled to explain your 'past' to yourself, can you escape 'the past' that you yourself have created? Can you shift this collection of bubbles? In fact, at the level of personal event bubbles this is an important part of what happens in a healing session. I guide the client in re-examining and re-experiencing key events, because the event bubbles that come up in a session always have some unresolved issue or unreleased feeling associated with them. Often these issues are unresolved because the event was overwhelming or because there was no time to process what was happening. These event bubbles then can be a major influence on the client's life with the unresolved issue trying desperately hard to find an outlet to be expressed in the present. Sometimes the event bubbles are unconscious—and they still have the power to influence us. These unconscious bubbles can even hold suppressed events, especially childhood events that we have strong reasons not to remember. Then too, the unconscious event bubble can be from a past life, and it influences the client to repeat or to avoid situations that are analogous to the past life.

As a healer, one way that I handle such past life influences during a healing session is to help you, my client, to 'reframe' an event bubble so that you can consciously choose an alternative meaning for the event. As a Creator Being you have the ability to reconsider the event and to give power to the alternative version that overwrites the original. We want the original event bubble to loose its power to influence you—we want the event to become neutral. That means clearing limiting thoughts and feelings about the event. And in truth, this process of 'reframing' event bubbles is something that people are doing all of the time as part of their natural growth process. People are often revisiting the bubbles of the past, rethinking the events, and reframing their core meanings. When as an adult you revisit your childhood memories with your parents, and you begin to understand your parents' actions from an adult point of view, then you are changing the essential meaning of what is held in your childhood event bubbles. You have entered into the bubble and used your creative power to reorganize its content. When you revisit the death of a person close to you that had seemed premature or unnecessary, and you are able to release your sadness and to see that death in a larger context, then you transform the core meaning of the bubble for that event and move toward a place of neutrality.

We are all growing and changing as we reframe the meanings held in our event bubbles. In fact, one might say that individually and collectively we are changing ourselves in the present by changing our past. The facts of the past may seem indisputable, but how you interpret those facts is the aspect of history that matters the most. So, what then do you make of 'the past' and 'memories of the past'? The notion that history is a timeline and that one historical event causes another—these are concepts that we have inherited. They are learned concepts that we superimpose on our fragmentary mental imagery to help us make sense of it. But there are numerous communities of indigenous peoples whose languages don't have a past tense, and they seem to get along just fine without our notion of the historical past! Maybe what we call 'our past' is really our present.

Just how much your ideas about your past and your recollections of your past are essentially your own construction is revealed by how narrowly focused these recollections are. When you recollect the past, you don't really re-enter a previous point in time. No, what you do is assemble and rehearse a sequence of event bubbles—fragmentary images and thoughts in the order and organization in which you have decided to hold them. Psychologists recognize that we often reshape our memories to meet our present needs. There is always some intention, conscious or unconscious, to make better sense of it all, and maybe to change those parts of the past that we would rather not deal with. So, all of this is to say that 'the past' doesn't exist in any real sense other than the one in which we choose to actively assemble 'the past' in the present moment when we perform the task of remembering. The past is simply the way that you fill in the blanks in our concept of 'the past,' a process that you perform in the present. The absolute truth of 'the past' just doesn't stand up under cross-examination. When we look at it all from this perspective, it is downright amazing that we don't immediately see that our notions of 'the past' are essentially just reflections of ourselves in the present—just like our 'historical' movies.

You must come to understand the finite nature of your bubbles. Every bubble has a limited scope, and so it is absolutely true to say that every bubble is inherently incomplete—and it probably contradicts some other bubble. It is no surprise that contradictions among the bubbles can lead to lifetimes of struggle to reconcile what one inherits from these bubbles with the reality that you experience in everyday life. Your bubbles may be necessary for making sense of the world, but at the same time they are suspect and never to be mistaken for absolute truth. Bubbles are just bubbles.

Changing Our Everyday World

Once you discard the weight of your 'past,' the present moment is full of new and interesting possibilities. Just think: you might see your everyday life in a context of divine beauty and grace. You might find yourself in great spiritual bubbles of broad perspective and deep understanding. You could even help build a better collective reality. But before you can really take advantage of your expanded creative capacity, you need to take control of where you direct your energy, and you need to be conscious about making changes. If you look all around, you can see that people are already constantly evolving. Everyone is undergoing change and transformation as they adapt to the shifting circumstances of their lives. Change is constant. What change shall you choose? The point is not that you should live without bubbles; you need your bubbles to make sense of the world. But you have choices to make about which bubbles you give your energy to and what is most important to you in your life. Once you understand that bubbles are as real as planes, trains, and automobiles, then you have a definite advantage in making decisions and recreating your world in a conscious way.

In truth, to go beyond the limited horizon of your old collective bubbles, you must move into a space that lies beyond them and to see your situation from a different perspective. That undoubtedly means finding a point of view outside of the old collective bubble from which you want to escape. The first step is knowing that you want to change. The second is to experience your situation from outside of the bubble and to hold onto your new perspective. You may have a moment of self-revelation or maybe someone outside of the bubble helps you to see your situation. But once that has happened, the motivation to break free of dysfunctional collective bubbles and to create a better life becomes strong and inevitable. As Divine Creator said back at the beginning: "You'll figure out the rest." You already know that you can do this!

Chapter 16 — Through the Lens

People use the word 'consciousness' in a lot of different ways, most of which are probably a little different from the way I am using the word here. One of these uses is in phrases like 'his consciousness' or 'her consciousness,' which suggest that the qualities of consciousness vary from one person to the next. And, of course, people also say things like consciousness is 'higher' or 'lower,' or 'stronger' or 'weaker.' All of these phrases certainly mean something, but do they mean exactly what they literally say? What I think is that people are actually describing an overall impression of the flow of consciousness. It is really about the patterns through which consciousness flows, not the consciousness itself. To me, consciousness is fluid, and consciousness itself is a fundamental phenomenon. There isn't actually 'higher' or 'lower' consciousness. Consciousness just is. Fundamentally, it is Divine Creator's consciousness. But we do create patterns for the flow of consciousness that have different qualities that we can experience and describe with words like 'higher' or 'lower.' These patterns can be quite steady and give the impression of something that is solid and stable. The solidity actually comes from the bubbles that hold boundaries around these patterns and stabilize the flow of consciousness.

We could also say that bubbles with their boundaries are like a lens through which we focus on the world around us. Bubbles bring into focus some perceptions, while excluding others—just like the lens of a camera. We might also describe the lens as being like colored glass that only allows a particular color of light to pass through it. Put on blue-tinted sunglasses, and you live in a blue world that excludes red and green. Connect yourself to a bubble of hopelessness, and everything around you is hopeless. Bubbles filter your perception of the world around you in a way that is both like a lens and like colored glass. But a bubble is even more than these because it also supplies a context around what we perceive. The focusing effect of a bubble is not just the 'what' but also the 'what about.' It connects things together in a larger pattern. This is what we discussed earlier in terms of schemas. In matching our perceptions to a pattern, the schema can also fill in the missing pieces. If we catch a glimpse of a car, we immediately know things about the car that we didn't see in the eye's passing moment. It is a powerful effect: when connecting to the bubble for 'car,' a huge network of bubbles is activated, and consciousness experiences a passing glimmer as 'car.'

Then too, when something really novel enters into our field of perception, we usually try to grasp it in terms of what is already familiar to us. We search for whatever bubbles would help us to understand and explain what this new thing is and how it fits into our world. Even if there isn't a bubble that exactly matches the new situation, there is usually some bubble or combination of bubbles that are close enough to make some kind of sense of the situation. We might have to stretch our bubbles a bit or throw things together in some new combination. Obviously then, making sense of all the various things we encounter in a single day is a dynamic process that takes a lot of bubbles. And we need many networks of bubbles and their schemas to make sense of our world as a whole—to create the apparent reality that we each experience.

Without the lens of the bubble, all perception would be blurry and unorganized. Or, if we can't match the new event with any established bubbles, then we might not be able to perceive anything at all! Now this point of view might sound quite extreme when talking about the physical world. But even our perception of physical reality may not be as objective and automatic as you first think. Yes, physical objects are 'real,' and our physical senses are responding to 'real' sensations, but what we make of those sensations is up to the bubbles. After all, to look at a 'chair,' we must already know what it is. A 'chair' is something that we sit on, and it has three or more legs and a back, and etc. If you had arrived from some other universe where you had never seen a chair, then a 'chair' is a strange looking object indeed. You might think, "What a strange object! Whatever does it do?"

The idea of 'the bubble as lens' is probably more obvious when talking about the world of spirit. After all, spiritual phenomena are seldom seen with the physical eyes, and people express a lot of different opinions about what is perceived in the spiritual realms. In the case of spiritual perception, it is easy to understand that the bubble plays an essential role in clarifying our extrasensory perception—bringing into focus some things while excluding others. Maybe while clarifying what is present, bubbles are also filling in the organization of our spiritual world.

Maybe focusing on physical 'things' all of the time distracts us from how we are constantly shifting our consciousness from the bubble of one thing to another. In truth, the physical world only appears as stable and predictable as it does because we are responding to it over and over again through the lenses of the same collective bubbles. A rose is a rose, but there is also a shared feeling and understanding that we have created around 'roses.' There may be a great many individual experiences of roses, but they are likely all grounded in the same collective understanding of roses. And it is not just the small things, not just the little items we encounter everyday that we perceive through the lens of collective bubbles. Take in the big picture—the way we can understand the overall sense of how the world is put together—that is also coming to us through a collective lens. When you look at it this way, then there is not such a great difference between the influences of bubbles in everyday life and in spiritual life. In fact, there is no practical separation at all. All life is interpreted through the lens of a bubble.

Consciousness Requires Limitations

Bubbles are essential to making any sense of our perception, whether sensory or extrasensory, and, in fact, bubbles are an essential aspect of consciousness. Bubbles are what enable you to perceive and comprehend the spiritual world, but the consequence is that everything you take in comes to you through the lens of a bubble that has simplified and guided by your perception. The core truth is that the flow of consciousness requires limitations. Without limitations, one could not, would not, perceive anything other than disorganized energy. Without limitations one could not be able to sustain a consciousness that is individuated from All-That-Is. Individuated consciousness requires a lens.

The key role of bubbles in spiritual life, and more specifically the role of the schemas embodied in the bubbles, has barely been acknowledged. There can be a great many things in the Cosmos that one could potentially perceive, but one can't see them at all without the lens of a bubble. Maybe you are attempting to perceive something that is quite multi-dimensional, and your third-dimensional mind can't grasp it. What can you perceive without some frame of reference, some organization to what your senses are providing you? Without the kind of lens that a bubble provides, you would not perceive angels or masters. There would be no spiritual levels, and the light-body would have no structure or meaning. You cannot comprehend what is beyond your perception's ability to grasp. Of course, something is there, but it is a phenomenon of energy or whatever you want to call it, and it is often multidimensional. You cannot interpret that energy without limiting it, simplifying it, and translating it. You need the lens of a bubble to give you something to hold onto.

So, if the bubble's schema is the lens through which spiritual perception is focused and organized, what is on the other side of the lens? If you should have the experience of an archangel, you do so through a lens of understanding that provides you with a context for archangels: images of archangels, an idea of what they do, the feeling of being in their presence, and possibly memories of past experiences with archangels. Otherwise, you might experience them as a more generic beneficial spirit, a deva or a god from another era, something for which you have a bubble. Once extrasensory perception activates the bubble's schema of the archangel, it also usually triggers the mental schema so that the mind has something to hold onto. The two kinds of schemas work together in concert to give focus, both psychic and mental, to the extrasensory perception. At the same time, this lens is clearly the creation of Creator Beings, and the structure that it imparts to your perception is the result of a creative act. And if all of this is a product of the lens, then what is one perceiving?

The deep truth is that you don't really know what is beyond the lens, and you cannot know. Your bubbles are your knowledge. You cannot 'know' anything without the limitation of the lens. If we believe that there is something there that exists in a form that we could describe as its 'true form' and genuine expression, then we can say that the bubble's schema is a lens of interpretation that provides us with a way of seeing it even though its 'true form' cannot be grasped. And still, our bubbles evolve and grow as we push the boundaries of our perception.

Creativity In Perception

Every act of perception contains an element of creativity. As Creator Beings, you literally create your way of perceiving the world. That is what you do—individually and collectively. In attempting to comprehend your experience, you expand the network of bubbles that makes sense of your experience. In this way, you can understand that the act of perceiving is the precise moment in which you create your world. You assemble it from bubbles. In the moment of perception, in the 'now,' there is access to the energy of unfolding creation in which the potential for change could become manifest. Maybe a new element of creation will be added to the bubble. Maybe elements of other bubbles combine to create a new combination. Perception is always a creative act, and those creative acts accumulate as you and others repeatedly reinforce and reinvent the network of bubbles.

Humanity has a relationship with the spiritual realms that is mediated by bubbles. At the same time, humanity has adopted very specific systems of mental schemas that embody the spiritual and religious teachings that shape how the mind understands those realms. The interconnection of these systems of mental schemas with the networks of psychic bubbles facilitates the creation of sacred texts and spiritual art. Most often, these words and images enable people to access spiritual knowledge and extrasensory perception in terms of forms and appearances that resemble the ordinary physical world. In our most common kinds of spiritual art, spiritual beings have physical bodies like human beings or like animals, and energetic objects behave like physical objects. Thus, a very sublime earth spirit may take the form of an eagle that can soar high in the sky, and angels have human bodies with wings that carry them between the world of spirit and the world of humanity on the earth. Archangel Michael even carries a very physical object: a sword.

There is an inner truth to these images, and at the same time we should remember that these images are the products of bubbles that enable and give a concrete shape to our perception. In their resemblance to the physical world, they are, of course, our own creation. We can embrace them as we embrace our own children, for they are ours—the result of our efforts to expand the range of our perception and awareness. The bubbles of spiritual schema have a power that is given to them by the Creator Beings who created them, but we should not mistake the schema for the energetic phenomenon it helps us to experience. As an example, think of the Hindu world's iconography and cosmology. There we find a network of spiritual beings, many of who are portrayed with human forms. Like many systems, it can be a self-contained and self-sufficient framework for spiritual consciousness. The Hindu field of schemas is a powerful one. Connecting to a larger spiritual world like this can be a very awakening experience that for many people expands the flow of consciousness into new patterns. For example, it can take people into reverence and awe beyond ordinary, everyday experience.

Our bubbles' schemas are intertwined with our mental schemas, one reinforcing the other. Our understanding of 'archangel' is both mental and psychic. And in this way the limitations of mental reasoning can come to interfere with psychic perception. The confusions created by people who mentally reason about the psychic realms are paramount. And here is an important lesson: we must avoid the compulsion to force our mental understandings onto our psychic perceptions. For example, if we fear what we might perceive, then we will effectively change what we see, by changing our bubbles. If there is an urgency within us to limit and rationalize our perceptions, then we will certainly make it happen by adjusting the lens of our bubbles. We will adjust our schemas to match what we think and feel that we need. Our active state of awareness steers our perceptions through the schemas that we have currently activated, whether we are in a place of neutrality or desperation. In that sense, our bubbles can cause our perceptions to reflect our inner state!

Evolutionary Consciousness

The evolution of consciousness can be viewed as the evolution of the bubbles that give shape to how our consciousness flows. The structure of a network of bubbles for a group of Creator Beings like us holds the collective patterns for the flow of our consciousness. This network of bubbles is like a scaffolding that guides consciousness along certain pathways and not others. You could say that we create a 'style of consciousness' that differentiates us as a group of Creator Beings from others, separates humans from groups of star people like the

Arcturians, and the degree to which we are able to communicate with star people depends on the extent to which we are able to access their style of consciousness as it is embodied in their network of bubbles.

And our consciousness evolves every time that we stretch our bubbles to embrace new perceptions that take us to the edge of our bubbles and every time that we merge bubbles to embrace a new possibility. Our bubbles expand through contact with spiritual beings and star people of other dimensions as we pick up and incorporate something of their style of consciousness. We are constantly evolving past the bubbles of our old spiritual systems and creating something that expands our spiritual possibilities.

And here is one of the great truths about Creator Beings: their greatest creation is the vast network of bubbles that capture their worldview with all of its diverse components. It is like a planet made of interconnected crystalline forms. That worldview captured in bubbles is as concrete a creation as a tall building or a city of light. This is the primary reason to be Creator Beings! It is not our monuments built in the physical world that matter most—it is what we have created in the unseen universe.

These networks of bubbles are another way in which Divine Creator expands the space of All-That-Is, in this case, by expanding the space of all possibilities for the flow of consciousness. Creator Beings work to expand the range of possibilities by creating local bubbles in which a limited reality is sustained and explored. Each limited reality is the manifestation of a possibility. The possibilities for the flow of consciousness expand and grow. There is constant invention and shifting. Bubbles are born, live, merge, divide, and eventually die.

In this way, we can view All-That-Is as a vast cluster of bubbles like the thought-forms around the head, maybe you could imagine it as the cluster of thought-forms around Divine Creator's head! The universe is invisibly subdivided into a nearly infinite number of separate realities sustained by networks of bubbles produced by Creator Beings who invent and sustain the flow of consciousness within entire worlds. Let go of thinking of the universe as only a space filled with physical matter. It is much more a space for the flow of consciousness through complex systems of bubbles.

Chapter 17 — The Story of Your Light-Body, Part III

Earlier on in this book, we began telling the story of how your light-body came to be the way that it is. That story began when some of the pure divine essence of creation became individuated, held in your Soul Matrix, and then anchored in the physical body. And the story unfolded further as the light-body formed around the Soul Matrix and adapted to being joined with the physical body. We described the chakras, as well as the etheric body, the Ka body, and the astral body, as outcomes of this process of adapting the higher-dimensional energies to the physical world. Focusing on this process of adaptation gave us a simplifying point of view on the complexity of the light-body, and it also reinforced our appreciation of how flexible and responsive the light-body is to its circumstances. So for example, the light-body can change in response to new developments in human consciousness.

And it might seem a bit presumptuous of me, but I would like to propose a change to one tradition of how we view the light-body. It is a change that I believe guides our view more in alignment with humanity's evolution to Oneness. This change involves how we view what are most often referred to as the 'subtle bodies' or 'higher bodies.' In this context 'subtle' means delicate or intangible, and 'higher' means higher in vibration than the physical body—both terms help us to understand this aspect of our light-bodies. These 'higher bodies' are distinct states of vibration that permeate and encompass the entire light-body.

While there is substantial agreement across many cultures about the primary chakras, there is rather less agreement about the higher bodies. And I am going to go out on a limb and say that the ways in which people describe the higher bodies are much more dependent on their culture and training than for other aspects of the light-body like the chakras. After all, the chakras are tightly interwoven with the physical body; so I think that everyone's perceptions arrive at a greater consensus. The higher bodies are probably better described as levels of vibration in the overall field, and how we experience them depends much more on how our expectations guide our perceptions.

Our perceptions are steered by the lens of the bubble that holds our model for understanding the higher bodies. However you were taught to perceive them, that is probably how you perceive and understand them now. For most people in healing traditions, their training was designed to give practical support to their healings. I was trained by Amorah Quan Yin to work with five bodies: the etheric, emotional, mental, spiritual, and astral bodies. The Ka body came up in other contexts. This organization of the five higher bodies has served the needs of my clients very well, in particular, because they can understand themselves in terms of the emotional, mental, and spiritual aspects of their lives. And conveniently, this framework overlaps many other healers' systems.

But I want to create an alternative bubble about the higher bodies, one that is proving more useful to me in relating the higher bodies to the life experiences of my clients. A shift in my personal viewpoint happened when I began to question the concept of the emotional and mental bodies as separate phenomena. My experience as a healer is that I don't experience anything emotional that doesn't also contain something mental, and nothing mental that doesn't also contain something emotional. I am not saying that the words 'emotional' and 'mental' don't have real meaning or that you can't see the emotional and mental bodies if you ask (just like you can see the 'pain body' or the 'fear body' if you ask). I am saying that the two are viewpoints on the same pattern of primary energy. For me, the framework of 'emotional' vs. 'mental' is a culturally based point-of-view that involves expectation and choice. You see through the lens of the bubbles that you choose. I want to make a different choice and to create a different bubble of understanding.

Higher Bodies As Partials

Stay with me now if this image seems a little humorous to you: but from one perspective, the energy body is like a really big resonant jar. If you strike such a jar or blow air across the top of it, you can imagine that it resonates with a sound. The bigger the jar, the deeper the sound. I want to draw an analogy between the vibrations of the light-body and the resonance of a really big jar.

The anchoring of the Soul Matrix in the physical body causes waves of energy to radiate through multi-dimensional space. The lowest of those waves radiates out and forms a multidimensional sphere centered around the Soul Matrix that is the outer boundary, the container of the light-body. And just like a jar, it holds a space in which many higher frequencies can resonate.

Blowing wind across the top of a big jar stirs the air inside the jar and creates the sound resonating from within the jar. All jars resonate at one bass frequency and many higher frequencies above that—frequencies that in the field of acoustics are called the 'partials,' that is, the 'parts' of the sound. The strengths of these individual partials go up and down depending on the force and steadiness of the wind. But the sound they make is whole even if it is made up of many partials. For the light-body of a human being, we might say that wind is the energy of the Cosmos and the Earth moving all around and through us that animates our lives. That wind is changing all the time and affecting the 'sound' that we radiate out into the world. In this way, we are forced to adjust and adapt to the constant shifts in the flow of energy. You can feel how the energy changes from one day to the next.

The partial frequencies of the light-body are to me the vibrations of the higher bodies—vibrations that stretch from the lowest bass frequency of our outer container up into higher frequencies that ultimately blend with Oneness. The frequencies of the higher bodies can each be experienced individually, rather like listening to one line of music in a choir of voices. Each one is adapting in its own way to the on-going resonance of the light-body and to the influences of the physical body. In this view, we can imagine that each higher body starts off as a pure pitch that responds to the influences of the moment, most importantly to the stream of energies blowing across the top of the jar. This is the pristine starting point at which adaptation begins to shape the relationship of these frequencies to life in the physical world and to the influences of human culture. It is the adaptation that leads to what we experience as the individual higher bodies. It seems a beautiful analogy to me that the higher bodies are the 'partials' of the whole, because we retain a sense of our wholeness like a melody that is expressing the song of our life.

The Four Bodies Fundamental to Being Human

So, we want now to describe the light-body's individual partials in terms of how biological consciousness joins with Higher-Self consciousness. I want to start with the lowest and the most fundamental of all the partials, the one that we will call the **Life Body**. It is the fundamental vibration of the joining of pure soul essence with biological life, the fundamental bond. It holds the resonance of 'I exist,' the core of being individuated in a finite, physical world. Its impulse is to insure our survival through the predominance of our physical nature in the balance between Earth and Cosmos. It holds the boundaries of the light-body in a coherent form and is the container of Qi and Ka empowering the potential expression of the Higher Self in an embrace of physical life.

The resonance of the Life Body is connected to the central channel through the root chakra. In this sense the root chakra is the anchor point at which the Life Body directly connects the light-body with the physical body. Any disruptions of the Life Body cause malfunctions in the organization of the rest of the light-body, but it is only disrupted when the stability of our relationship to life is disrupted, because then the light-body system can begin to break down.

The higher bodies' adaptation to the physical body continues with the vibration of each partial frequency, and each partial expresses its own unique relationship between our life on the physical plane and our life as spiritual beings. Each has an anchor point in a major chakra. In fact, viewing the connection between the higher bodies and the chakras in this way helps us to understand how each chakra and body holds a unique quality of our greater consciousness—truly just like the analogy of how white light is composed of individual colors. The wellspring of our flowing consciousness is our light-body in its entirety. We are really describing one integrated system—the light-body and how it expresses the nature of a human being. I think that the differences between how we describe the chakras and how we describe the higher bodies are largely the result of cultural influences that hide their pure nature from our view. What I want to capture here is a framework that helps to guide human evolution in harmony with Oneness. I think that by changing our framework—by shifting to a different bubble—we create a more holistic understanding of ourselves.

The next higher partial in sequence and the one associated with the second chakra we will call the **Primal Body**. The 'Primal Body' is a level of vibration that is more individual and personal. It holds the resonance that 'I' and 'my body' are one. You can think of the Life Body and the Primal Body together as representing the foundation of biological consciousness in our light-body. As a level of pure vibration, the Primal Body resonates with the slowest changes that are experienced by the physical body. In particular, it resonates with bodily sensation and feeling, which is why this body is often associated with emotions—but only a particular range of emotions. Its state usually reflects an assessment of individual wellbeing, as in 'does something affect me positively or negatively' and 'how strong is it'? These aspects of assessing individual wellbeing are both elements of perception and communication—our perception of how the world around us affects us and our communication that affects the world. Dysfunctions of the Primal Body tend to involve negative assessments that accumulate to the point that the individual is overwhelmed in negativity. This is also the body that most often holds an individual's core anxiety. That anxiety typically took shape during the early stages of life during which the individual manifested bubbles in the light-body that hold the child's negative experience. These bubbles are typically pre-verbal and deeply tied to bodily feelings, and this core anxiety is often extremely strong in only the way that a very young child could experience.

The next higher partial in the energy-body resonance gives rise to the **Tribal Body**. This level of vibration is connected to our wellbeing in relationship to other humans—others as in family and others as in tribe. It holds the resonance that 'I' and 'my tribe' are one—we are all in this life together. At the beginning of our lives, this level of vibration reaches out and resonates with our immediate family, which in hunter-gatherer times was integrated with the tribe. It becomes the foundational model for all our social relationships. Today, it expands from tribe to other groups around us. The Tribal Body is very influential in childhood as young people find their place among their peers. As we continue on through life, our primary relationships and how we understand our place in society are strongly shaped by what we hold in the Tribal Body. Disruptions here can produce alienation and loneliness on the one hand, and over-identification and submersion in the tribe on the other. Our challenge is to live in balance and harmony with our tribe and all its members. Through our psychic capacities, we perceive and we communicate with each other at this level of vibration. For most people, this connection is rich with feeling and strongly shaped by our collective consciousness, even when it is in a dysfunctional state. Easy to see that for many people today 'tribe' as a coherent unit of social organization is quite broken down. Just the same, we form relationships to 'our tribe' in whatever form we come to experience it.

I believe that there is an argument to be made that our

breakdown of tribal consciousness is a cause of instability in our romantic relationships. People are often looking for something in these relationships that no one person can possibly fulfill—they are looking for their 'tribe' but remain unfulfilled. Only a 'tribe' would give us the deep sense of personal completeness that we look for in most romantic relationships. Meanwhile, modern societies create a myriad of transitory and insubstantial substitutes for 'tribe' without creating personal fulfillment.

The next higher frequency brings us to a level that transcends the self and the tribe to the wellbeing of all. I think that it is best called the **Empathy Body**. The primary characteristic of this body's vibration is that it resonates transparently with everything else in our world. It holds the resonance that 'I' and 'all others' are one. Through this body, humans experience themselves as a part of everything in their world. All people are connected to each other, and all humanity is connected to the Earth. Especially too, the fundamental separation of 'I' and 'Thou' is broken down—there is no separation between ourselves and 'the other.' I believe that the focus of how this higher body adapts our higher-dimensional energies to our physical body is primarily in our transcendence of tribe and our embrace all of humanity, but also in our embrace of the Earth as a spiritual being. We experience ourselves as part of the larger web of life and we recognize our place within the web. There is a spontaneous expression of love that emerges when we experience 'I' and 'Thou' as one—thereafter, we long to stay in that state of love. The capacity of the Empathy Body to transcend limitation is also essential for Unity Consciousness. The more that we can liberate our vibration at this frequency, the more that the Empathy Body can help to loosen the blockages and dysfunctions of the three bodies below it—the unity of 'I' and 'Thou' takes us into unity with our tribe, our body, and our relationship to being alive.

In summary, here we see the foundations of how Higher-Self consciousness joins with biological consciousness:

Life Body   I exist
Primal Body   I and my body are one
Tribal Body   I and my tribe are one
Empathy Body   I and all others are one

Healing these Higher Bodies

When I am helping a client and working with these higher bodies, I am looking at each to see what blocks it from being in wholeness and health. I want to see the client in relationship to a fully functional and happy life. And as I become aware of whatever limitations are disrupting the client's life, the primary question for me focuses on: "What keeps this higher body in separation from Oneness?"

With each affected body, I run energy to heal the separation. Sometimes, I am shown specific blockages, dissociated consciousness, etc., and then I work to heal those. But in general, I am working from the outside the client's bubble to break down the client's limited reality. Where do these bubbles come from? Generally the client has created the limiting bubbles around this aspect of their life—limited in health and body, limited in their relationships to other people, or limited in love. Yes, there are collective supports, but my focus is to stop the client from supporting the bubble. They maintain their limited vision of themselves by giving energy to that vision. For example, they give energy to their vision of inadequacies and loneliness. But when they change the image, their energy moves to support a new image. They feed energy to a new bubble that they are creating—one that gives support to a life of wellbeing.

In this they are claiming their own sovereignty and freeing their capacity to express their true self.

Concerning the Emotional and Mental Bodies

You may still be wondering what happened to the traditional emotional and mental bodies in this new system. In this alternative view of the higher bodies, there are 'emotional' and 'mental' aspects potentially in each of the four bodies we have discussed. So, reactions to events that we might describe as 'emotional-mental' can be present in any or all of the first four bodies. For example, an experience of abandonment may give rise to a reaction in the Life Body of: "Will I survive?" The reaction in the Primal Body might be: "What does this mean to my well-being?" A reaction in the Tribal Body might focus on: "How does this affect my relationship with my tribe?" And in the Empathy Body, there could be a reaction like: "Is love gone?" Given the circumstances and the predisposition of a given person, any combination or all of these reactions might occur. Emotional and mental reactions occur simultaneously, and in truth they are fused together at the level of each body.

So, this takes us back to my earlier point that 'emotional' and 'mental' are interpretations of the same core energy structures. To this, I also want to add the observation that the emotional and mental aspects of a blockage cannot really be healed separately, and attempting to do so puts the client in a bubble of emotional-mental duality. The goal of the alternative viewpoint on the higher bodies is to always work on the light-body from the viewpoint of Oneness.

Breaking Bubbles

Chapter 17

The Bodies Of Our Cosmic Connection

I would like to just briefly comment on the higher bodies that continue on after the first four. These are bodies that resonate at the higher frequencies of the light-body's higher partials and are less connected to ourselves as Earthly beings, more to ourselves as Cosmic beings. Consider the first four bodies we have discussed. They themselves range from the most individual (Life Body and Primal Body) to the most collective and universal (Empathy Body). The Empathy Body and the heart chakra can be viewed as pivot points in our balance between Earth and Cosmos. The bodies of the higher partials are increasingly universal and represent more of our relationship to the Cosmos. That is one reason why divine surrender becomes such an important issue on our spiritual path—because in opening ourselves to Oneness we must learn how to balance our individuality with the universality of the Cosmos.

My teacher, Amorah Quan Yin, took the approach of addressing these higher bodies as a group and calling them the Spiritual Body. And that makes perfect sense to me as a way of addressing their focus and qualities from the perspective of a human life, because the sense of these bodies becomes more and more difficult to describe in everyday language. And for that reason I personally avoid descriptive labels, and I will just refer to them by number. They each retain a correspondence to the chakras, but I wouldn't extend the usual chakra descriptions to the bodies—those descriptions are just too cultural and too limited a point of view.

5th body—throat chakra
6th body—third eye chakra
7th body—crown chakra

And there are bodies beyond these just like higher states of vibration—pure and simple. It is best just to open yourself to their experience without trying to classify or hold onto anything. The experience itself is the form of knowledge that you need. True knowledge is knowing how to find your way through your pure intention.

Manifesting as a Pure Tone

The higher bodies are important to our capacities as Creator Beings. Our creative power emanates from the pure soul essence held in the Soul Matrix, and it resonates with the 'partials' of the light-body—just as if the light-body was a resonate jar producing a sound. The sound embodies a form, and the energy of unfolding creation organizes itself accordingly. It is really that simple.

But we are not all ready to resonate in that way. We must first clear our light-body of our mistuned energies, especially in the higher bodies and chakras. You might say that we have to clear ourselves of the acoustic bubbles that undermine our ability to vibrate as a pure tone. That clearing is a long-term process, a process by which we slowly bring our total vibration to a pristine state of purity.

And while we are evolving in that process, we have special centers in the palms of our hands that act to focus our creative capacities. These centers are typically called chakras, but despite being similar to chakras as complex centers of energy, we really ought to recognize them as something quite different. For lack of a more sophisticated name, we can simply call them the 'hand centers.' Their internal structure is specifically tailored to their role in sending and receiving multidimensional energy.

And in the same way that the physical hands are instruments by which we manifest in the physical world, the hand centers are instruments by which we manifest in the non-physical world. This is how our hands become our instruments of healing.

Our capacity as Creator Beings is vested through the wholeness of our light-body—all parts interconnected from micro to macro. This is what we are made to be. We hold a vision of what we intend to create, and we use our capacities to transform and to manifest our visions. And in one sense then the goal of our evolution can be understood quite clearly: to bring everything that we are to a pristine state so that we vibrate like a pure tone, and thereby, to become fully empowered as Creator Beings who can manifest with power and authority. To become a pure tone, we hold a vision of how our light-bodies might be—without mistunings. This is a vision for a human being who vibrates in harmony with Oneness.

Chapter 18 — Breaking Bubbles

Breaking Free Of Everyday Consciousness

Each day, our consciousness is flowing through the bubbles that sustain us while our thoughts and feelings follow the familiar patterns of everyday life. Almost all people have their attention primarily focused on ordinary stuff—those things and actions that seem perfectly normal and that seem to move along day after day in an inevitable flow. It all appears so stable and so ordinary, and there is a certain comfort to be found in the everyday flow of consciousness, a comfort that can hide the greater spiritual significance of our lives from us. This is one way in which the power of our consciousness can become dissipated and maybe even squandered because our attention is captured by our everyday reality. That is how our power to direct our lives can be so easily dissipated, and our consciousness lost in a maze of everyday bubbles with one leading to the next and the next . . ..

But 'you' are not wholly defined by your bubbles. 'You' are far, far more. For example, your divine soul essence is something entirely different from your bubbles, and it is always outside of the space enclosed by your bubbles. Your inner Divine Light opens into a wholly different reality from the reality created by your bubbles, and it always connects you back to your divine origins in Oneness. You are so much more than your everyday reality can hold. Stepping outside the narrow viewpoint of your everyday reality, the greater spiritual significance of 'you' can be a revelation. 'You' are a divine being of divine origins walking the Earth. This is true in every moment of your life—even when you are off shopping at the supermarket!

So, lets take a step back to look at this. As we have said before: here you are suspended between Earth and Cosmos—we might just as well have said suspended between an everyday life with its dull routines and a spiritual life that is filled with deep significance! As a human being striving to actualize the rich spiritual significance of your life, you need to break free of the everyday bubbles that tie your consciousness into that dull everyday world. You need to find your path through its confusing distractions to discover what is truly spiritually beneficial for you. You need to fill the gap between your everyday life and the potential of your spiritual life—to create a bridge for your consciousness between what your life is now and what you can envision for yourself.

And so now we come to a core question: once you recognize that your bubbles have trapped your consciousness in everyday routines, how will you take control of your evolution and fulfill your goal of having a spiritually rich and meaningful life? We all have choices that we can make about our relationship to change in our lives. But how do you learn to break and remake the bubbles that will redirect the flow of your consciousness?

Yes, your bubbles are containers for patterns of consciousness, and they contain what you put into them at the moment of their creation. Bubbles of everyday consciousness are just that: bubbles of everyday consciousness. Where you direct your attention and energy, that is exactly where your consciousness flows. To experience the possibilities of bubbles beyond that level of everyday consciousness, you need to invest energy in those aspects of your life that you want to enhance. This is one way that you begin to create bubbles that guide your spiritual evolution in new directions.

Here is a small, concrete example of breaking a limiting bubble and replacing it with new bubble that is worth giving your energy to. Almost all spiritual traditions use 'height' as a metaphorical to express levels of spiritual evolution. That metaphor gives us 'higher consciousness' and 'higher realms.' In the literal sense of this metaphor, heaven is above us, masters ascend, and advanced spiritual beings can fly. All of this makes metaphorical sense for 3D beings bound to the Earth by gravity. And I have employed this metaphor in some of our preceding discussion, because it is part of the common spiritual vocabulary. But this metaphor creates an illusion of distance between us and 'higher consciousness' and 'higher realms.' If there is height, there is distance, and distance means separation. But what if there is no separation? After all, 'distance' is a concept based on living in the 3D world where physical distance is a reality. What if 'distance' at other levels of consciousness is a misunderstanding? Maybe we have dragged our concept of 'distance' with us into planes of consciousness where it doesn't belong? If that is true, then the concept of spiritual height collapses. What if there were no higher realms laid one on top of the other? No distance to transverse.

What if everything is here right now—around you and within you in the present moment?

Indeed, this concept is the more illuminating truth. Step out of any old thinking that the spiritual life that you long for is separated from you, or that it requires effort to get there, or that Divine Creator is somewhere beyond your reach (and maybe needs to send you an invitation to have coffee). There is no separation. Everything you need is here right now. Really embrace this truth. There is nowhere to go.

If you follow this shift of perspective when reading this, you have broken through one bubble and shifted into a new one. You are looking through a different lens. This is a bubble that is in alignment with the greater truth of Oneness—the Law of One. From the perspective inside of this bubble, the proposition that you are separated from the world of spirit, separated from your Higher Self, or separated from Divine Creator is preposterous—obviously wrong. There is no separation outside of your bubble that holds the illusion of separation. Time to break that bubble forever.

Nobody would likely choose to keep their consciousness tangled up in their old everyday reality if they were looking at this big picture. But alas, we are usually looking through the lens of our everyday reality at the small picture. It is not so much 'what' we focus our attention on, as it is 'how' we focus our attention, because even the everyday physical world can be experienced through a lens that reveals the eminent presence of Oneness—everything is here now. Right here, right now—even in the physical world.

We need to devote our energy to the bubbles that connect us most directly to Oneness. These bubbles by their inherent nature then will transform our experience of everyday life. Lets set our sights right now on living in an everyday world that emanates Oneness. Clearly, any bubbles that steer the flow of our consciousness away from Oneness need to be broken down and replaced by bubbles that open up new possibilities for experiencing Oneness in our lives. Everyone experiences the universal impulse to liberate their consciousness and to explore beyond the limits of their present reality—to rejoin the unlimited consciousness beyond all bubbles. Our challenge is to create bubbles that are in greater and greater harmony with

Oneness at the same time that Oneness may seem beyond the scope of our understanding.

"We ask that the seed of Oneness be planted within us to guide our evolution into ever greater harmony with Oneness."

Step One: Readiness

Whatever our life's situation and however far we have come on our spiritual path, we need readiness in order to proceed. It is not to be taken for granted. If you hold onto doubt that things can really change, you need to cancel such beliefs right now. Ideally, we might want to make readiness a part of our life's dedication to our spiritual work, but we can't always be in a state of readiness, and we can't always anticipate what we will need to be ready for. Sometimes the readiness that we need in order to take the next step in our lives arrives unexpectedly. It comes in the form of people who awaken something within us. It comes in the shape of events that shake up our lives and dismantle our coping mechanisms. And maybe it comes quietly like a hushed voice telling us that there is something more. There are a thousand paths to readiness, but without readiness you are resisting your own evolution.

I feel lucky when I meet my clients, because I know that on some level they have already made the decision to change their lives. And clients almost always have some ideas about how they want to change. Maybe they just don't know quite how to do it, and maybe they need some help in fully accepting new possibilities for themselves. Even still, I often ask my clients directly if they are ready to make the changes that they need. I know that they are going to answer 'yes', but what I am seeking is an opportunity for them to focus their intention and to empower their choice to change—"Yes, I am ready to let go and embrace change." We all need to invest our energy in changing.

But even my clients who are walking the path of healing differ in their levels of readiness. It seems that many people are in constant negotiation with themselves about change. The negotiation is about exactly what and how much they are ready for—often, how much they can manage without feeling overwhelmed. A familiar example happens with relationships. Maybe this is your experience too, but people usually know deep within themselves that they need to leave a relationship long before they finally find the will and clarity to do it. Other life changes can be just like that: Are we ready to leave our relationship with our old self? Are we ready to listen to our inner guidance? All of this has an element of uncertainty to it, because when we choose change, we seldom comprehend fully what it will mean for us. But the negotiation is an important step.

The reasons why a person resists readiness and holds onto their limiting situation can be complex. There is often a phase of resistance during which lots of reasons for not changing come up: "My boyfriend is not interested in what I am interested in" or "I can't tackle any changes right now because of my situation at work." And this might seem an extreme example, but I also see clients who experience physical pain but who are not ready to let go of it. In the case of my clients, we are generally talking about pain that has its root in issues of the light-body. The clients say that they want to get rid of the pain, and at the same time they don't want to let go of something that having the pain supports. The negotiation for the client revolves around the question of how exactly are they benefiting from their pain. Maybe the pain is helping the client to avoid some action—like standing up for themselves in a key relationship or accepting some difficult truth about their lives. Possibly too, there are multiple factors holding the pain in place. These contrary motivations need to be released before a dysfunctional bubble around the pain can be completely collapsed. But readiness doesn't require absolute clarity. You simply need to be ready to move on from the situation that you are in.

Step Two: Breaking the Bubble

The path of healing is an on-going process of bringing change into your life by breaking bubbles. At its core, breaking bubbles removes the separations that keep you out of harmony with Oneness. In my experience every person needs healing in order to be ready for the awakening of Oneness. In fact, I think that without personal healing you will always discover yourself held back in your spiritual development by personal issues that might otherwise be totally invisible to you. No matter how many hours you practice meditation or how many good acts you perform, you can't avoid the step of healing yourself. 'You' are your primary responsibility. And you can't simply shift the focus outside of yourself by helping others or living a proper life. You must liberate yourself from your compulsions and dysfunctional patterns, and then all of the other changes and development you want in your life can flow from that.

We already know a great deal about breaking bubbles from our discussion of the path of healing. That discussion focused on ways of collapsing bubbles by healing what was on the inside, for example, releasing unexpressed emotions, canceling limiting beliefs, etc. And maybe it wasn't always obvious, but these healing techniques also introduce something into the bubble from outside the bubble—an alternative perspective that triggers the healing. This relationship of inside and outside the bubble is directly manifested in the relationship of the healer to the client. The client seeks help from the healer who is outside of the client's bubbles, and from that vantage point, the healer works to enter into the client's bubbles in order to break them. This helps to explain why the support of a spiritual community can be so important to us, because no one can see all their bubbles. We often need the help of companions who can see what we can't.

Otherwise, in healing yourself the first step to breaking a bubble is to shift your attention outside the bubble. That experience causes a shift of perspective—hopefully it breaks your inner gaze loose from its fixation on seeing things the same way as you always have from inside the bubble, and you discover yourself on the outside looking in. The shift of perspective might be intentional or accidental. Whichever it is, being on the outside enables you to then look at your bubble as an observer, and at that moment, it is as if you are in a different reality than the bubble, the reality of a more expansive bubble. You need to be ready to hold onto that moment when it occurs.

It can be a lot like waking up to the realization that you have been living your life inside of one room. At first you just didn't see the room because all of your attention was focused on the things inside the room—the 'this' and the 'that' of your everyday life. And then one day, you look out the window, and it dawns on you that you are living inside of a room. You have been cooped up inside this room, and you just didn't realize it. "Ah, its time to leave," you might say. So, you try to command the door to open, and sometimes that works—but most of the time it is impossible to command the door to open from inside of the room. In this way, being inside of the room is exactly like a prison—the key is on the outside. The best way to get out of your room is actually a kind of magic trick. Look out the window and maybe you see a tree. Imagine yourself next to that tree and sense what it must be like next to the tree. Be with the tree, and then the next thing you know is that you are on the outside with the tree looking back at the room in which you were held. Maybe you have never actually understood before that there was a room. But just like Dorothy in the Wizard of Oz, you only had to click the ruby slippers in order to leave. The secret to the magic is realizing that you always had the power to fly past these limitations.

So, what has kept you inside the room? The window was always there, but what has kept you from understanding your situation before you really looked out that window and realized that you were trapped? Certainly habit, and probably the fear of facing up to the reality of your situation. But then comes that moment of readiness when you do actually look out and something different clicks inside you. Maybe you don't even recognize the shift. Many times, it seems like luck or some subconscious guidance has led you to that moment in which your perspective changes. It was always possible, but then it happens. And finally seeing your bubble as an outside observer opens up the possibility that you really 'see' how you have been trapped.

Maybe you recognize your captivity as misguided or punitive or simply inconceivable. You may ask yourself, "Why did I believe that?" or "What was I doing there?" Dorothy eventually wakes up to the fact that her experience of Oz was a dream, but it is nearly impossible to recognize a dream from inside the dream.

As long as you are trapped inside the bubble, its reality dominates and controls. So, you need to step back and look at your situation. Having the idea of your bubble's existence can probably get you started, but it is almost always being present to something outside of your bubbles that does the trick—to open to a more expansive view. After all, bubbles are about separation. You need to break down the separation that maintains the bubble's limited reality.

Nature. Connecting with nature can have this effect. It is one of the most direct ways of taking yourself to a space outside of your bubbles. But you need to be really present in Nature, not just skipping across the landscape. Give it your attention. This is a large part of why people make so many spiritual pilgrimages to special places in the natural world. When you really connect to the natural world, you are outside of the bubble of your everyday life and able to see your routine behaviors from a different perspective. Maybe you are able to see your everyday life without the sense of compulsion that keeps you caught up in doing things that make you unhappy. Your unhappiness is telling you that something is missing or out of alignment. But being present in Nature gives you a place to be away from those feelings and to reflect. Being in Nature can be a perfect foil to your everyday compulsions. Maybe you say to yourself, "I've been in denial" or "I can't keep driving myself like this."

Maybe being in Nature is so effective because when you are really open to see Nature as it is, you discover how much of your thinking and behavior are out of alignment with it. Nature doesn't hold on to pain or resentments or false beliefs. Nature doesn't feel pressured to be something that it isn't. The Earth simply is, and all Nature is indeed in constant transformation—living and dying. These are important lessons to learn. Nature's truth can have a very strong impact when you are trying to hold onto dysfunctional fantasies about yourself and your world.

I want to add my observation that a great deal of the negativity in the world today is a direct result of a lack of right relationship with the Earth. Our relationship with the Earth should hold an active balance of giving and receiving. We need to be giving and receiving nourishing energies with the Earth. Otherwise, we create a void within ourselves that negativity will fill. Part of the problem with everyday patterns of consciousness is the lack of connection to the Earth. And this is an area in which modern societies have much to learn from our ancestors and from indigenous peoples. Only when we live in right relationship with the Earth do we discover what it really means to be in balance between the Cosmos and the Earth.

Meditation. Another way to step outside the limited reality of your bubbles is to meditate and intentionally shift the flow of your consciousness to bubbles beyond your limitations. This means redirecting your awareness to the bubbles that connect you to the greater spiritual reality of your life. Those bubbles are the ones that lead you into greater and greater harmony with the Oneness.

Having a personal practice of meditation provides you with a technique for collapsing bubbles that you can use in daily life. The technique is simple. Move yourself into that 'state of consciousness' in which you meditate, and then reflect on the bubbles that control your life. Be the observer. Of course, most of the time, what the mind wants to focus on are the specific issues, the limitations inside of the bubbles. Don't step into them. Observe them from the outside and avoid moving into their emotions. For example, if you are stuck in a bad job, don't go into your desperate feelings about how you have no options—just observe yourself and your patterns. If you are experiencing pain because you think that you failed someone, don't go into experiencing the pain. Instead focus on being in that place that your meditative practice takes you. This is the place where the desperation and pain can dissolve, not because you have covered it over, but because in a more expansive *state of consciousness*, the narrative about your suffering has no traction.

There is no real mystery to what people mean by a 'state of consciousness.' It is essentially an overall impression of the bubbles your consciousness is moving through. If your consciousness is only flowing through the bubbles of fear, that is where your consciousness is—in a state of experiencing fear. And if your consciousness is flowing through bubbles that connect you to the greater spiritual meaning of your life, that is where your consciousness is. It is so simple: your state of consciousness is exactly where your consciousness flows.

But when we describe our 'states of consciousness,' we often talk about them as if they were places. Your everyday bubbles can make you feel that you are stuck in one place, and your meditation takes you to another place. That is an important power of a meditative practice. You can return to a state of consciousness that you choose. But in truth, your state of consciousness is under your control at all times, even in everyday life. So here is a suggestion for managing things: you can establish your 'preferred state of consciousness.' With practice, you simply 'travel' there when you choose. Carry this practice with you into everyday life so that you can take your healing practice with you and break bubbles as situations arise.

There is a special place that meditation can take you. It is variously called the 'great silence,' the 'place of emptiness,' the 'plain of nothingness,' etc. This is the place in which the chatter and compulsions of your everyday mind come to a dead halt, and you can experience an absence of limiting bubbles. This place is like a graveyard for bubbles because the illusory realities contained within bubbles cannot persist in the silence. Bubbles break open in the free and open space of absolute quiet.

Un-creating. With practice too, a very direct way to break bubbles is to 'un-create' them. We certainly have less practice at that than in creating them, but view 'un-creating' bubbles as simply the flip side of the coin. There is a technique. Create the opposite of the bubble you want to break, and bring the two bubbles together—you will figure out how. They can't co-exist with each other. If something survives the collision, create another opposite bubble and do it again. But be creative and do not hold on to limitations about the things that you un-create, because you might end up creating something else that is limiting to you. Remember to focus on what you want to accomplish by this act of un-creation; you want to create a clear space for yourself that is free of limitations—like the open space of absolute quiet.

Step Three: Through the Space of the Soul

All of these 'techniques' share the same essential core. They are all approaches to one key transaction. There is a special moment—maybe the same moment when you really see your bubble from the outside—when a fundamental thing is able to happen. It is the singular moment when we as Creator Beings break the bubble by passing it through the space of the soul. Even if we experience the bubble as something foreign and outside of ourselves, this transaction effectively occurs within us. You might say that the Divine Light of the soul is like a flame that burns away anything that is out of alignment, that which is in untruth.

And now it's time to expand our concepts a bit, because when we say that we 'break bubbles,' that is just a way of talking, a kind of 3D metaphorical communication. In order to reach a deeper understanding of how we actually break bubbles, we need to let go of this physical metaphor about 'bubbles' and to connect to something that is beyond the limitations of 3D thinking. The greater power to break bubbles comes from removing the separations, you could say by eliminating the 'boundedness' of the bubbles. When bubbles become unbounded, they lose their borders and the separation disappears. The creation of a bubble was an act of limitation, and the breaking of bubbles is an act of 'un-limitation.' There is a higher dimensional reality to what is going on. The bubble 'breaks' because at a higher dimensional level it is shifted to the unbounded space within the Soul Matrix. And there in the Divine Light of the soul—in the Oneness of the pure soul essence—there is no separation and the bubble cannot hold its separateness.

We can add to this understanding the fact that bubbles embody whatever was put into them at their creation. If they are created at a certain dimensional level, then that is their level. If they are created with a sense of loss and illusory beliefs based on limitations of 3D reality, then that is what they contain. The boundaries of these bubbles define the limits of the bubble's reality. Almost all are within the reality of time and space. Step out of that bubble and into the space of the Soul Matrix, then time and space disappear. When a bubble is brought into no-time and no-space, its low-dimensional borders of separation disappear.

This can help us to understand the moment in which you experience the breaking of a bubble. Because when a bubble breaks, there is a realignment of energies at multiple levels. There is a kind of automatic self-correction. Something less limiting that the bubble takes over and gives rise to a feeling of release. I could describe it as a feeling of something squeezed expanding into openness. It is a good feeling. When your attention is focused on yourself as a physical being, then you may feel this in your heart. And when your attention is centered in the space of your heart, you might experience this event as an expansion of love. The multidimensional space of the Soul Matrix is the place in which all healing ultimately occurs. But this event does not take place simply because you think it. It needs to take place as an action in unity with your Higher Self. You can become better and better at this the more in alignment with your Higher Self you are.

Step Four: Meeting our Truth on the Other Side

We have all stood at the doorstep of personal change, and we have all experienced passing through that doorway—sometimes passing into a better place within ourselves and sometimes finding ourselves face-to-face with challenges that we can't ignore. The ever-evolving path of your spiritual growth leads you through one doorway after another. Each doorway is like a portal that carries you from a familiar place to an unfamiliar place. That is indeed what marks progress on your spiritual path; it is a path of change and transformation, not only for your light-body, but importantly for the bubbles that hold together your viewpoint on the world around you. You evolve as your bubbles evolve. On the other side of the doorway is always the spirit of someone unfamiliar to you. That person is 'you' as you have never seen yourself before. It is indeed the beginning of a new relationship with yourself.

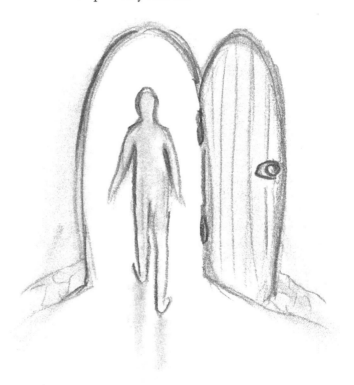

And there is often a reaction that takes hold sometime after you have walked through the doorway—where you discover yourself in a strange land. A strange land? Quite often it is a land in which you are not who you thought you were. Maybe you discover that your negative beliefs about yourself have kept your inner Divine Light hidden from you. Maybe you have to face up to your capacity to live a better life than you have attempted before—to step out of the pattern of disappointing yourself.

When this happens, it means that the bubbles that shaped your reality have changed.

Fear often comes in when you face the unfamiliar or unexpected, even if you are facing something unexpectedly positive. What you might be afraid of is the shocking realization that you are indeed a spiritual being and that your life is totally about your spiritual evolution. But there is nothing really to fear when you step through the doorway. Consider the stories of near-death experiences when people have walked through that most important doorway. These stories reveal an absence of fear—we don't seem to fear when we have left of our bodies. Out of the body, we can only understand fear as something belonging to the physical world.

This business of experiencing changes in your life does not always take you immediately to a better place. The passage through the portal always involves leaving one bubble and entering another. The bubble you break may be one that has hidden some truth from you, and the person who you meet on the other side of the portal may be yourself revealed in the light of a different truth. We all live in bubbles that hide some inner truth from ourselves. For example, we may think that we are strong and forceful, only to discover the truth that we have essentially been reacting out of our insecurity and weakness.

I remember one client who was very engaged in giving help and doing things for others, both at work and in his circle of friends. In a healing session after a crisis in his life, he recognized and came to grips with the realization that he had subtly controlled and manipulated the people around him through his supposed kindness. It was a coping mechanism that he had developed early on when growing up in his 'unsafe' family where he had learned to win favor and avoid the emotional abuse that was heaped on his siblings. Beneath his adult efforts in taking care of others, he was rebuilding the same zone of safety around himself that he created as a child. He was acting out of fear. Recognizing this aspect of himself was an important act of self-honesty and a necessary step toward clearing his pattern of hiding his fear behind a mask that had plagued his whole life—and had eventually led to his crisis. The old bubble in which he had seen himself as a kind and altruistic person had hidden his issues from him, and his new bubble enabled him to connect to a deeper truth. First of all, he needed to forgive himself and to open the way to loving himself despite his imperfections. Second, he had to open himself to feeling his fear and insecurity, to recognize it in his everyday life, and to not push it aside. It was then that his true loving feelings for others could be liberated. He truly was a loving person. On the other side of his portal, he discovered a person capable of truly balanced relationships with others, instead of the person who hid from his fears. But it took some time to come to grips with a lifetime's patterns of living from a place of insecurity. It took time to develop this new bubble that was in alignment with his true self.

Oneness Is a Process

The word 'Oneness' is a noun. And using that word over and over again in talking about spiritual life can lead to a misimpression: a misimpression that Oneness is something fixed and static. When we reduce Oneness to an abstraction that exists somewhere beyond the reach of our real lives, it looses its power and its significance. But despite the risk of creating something limited and disempowered out of something infinite and liberating, we need to hold onto this word and to penetrate its core meaning.

We are in the process of *"Awakening Oneness."* From the very beginning of this book we have treated Oneness as an awakening state of being, a state of being that is accessible to you and to everyone. It lies just below the surface of your everyday reality—it's just a matter of your breaking some bubbles. In this process of breaking bubbles there is the automatic self-correction that seems to take place like magic— you will establish a connection to new and more expansive bubbles. When you break an old bubble, there is always an enclosing bubble that offers you a new viewpoint on your situation. This bubble is a new starting point, a new part of the scaffolding that supports the expansion of your consciousness. Your new bubble is typically a bubble that has already been created and reinforced by other Creator Beings on their path of healing—it is part of humanity's spiritual legacy. Something new is formed in the wake of your broken bubbles.

So, in this sense Oneness is a process. When you reach out for that state of being, Oneness clarifies and remakes. There is no greater technique for breaking bubbles than this: to reduce each and every thing to Oneness. Reduce your work to Oneness, your life and tribulations reduce to Oneness, the energy of pain and separation reduce to Oneness. Oneness disassembles the complex and makes simple. Whatever is left after the complex is removed, that is something you have created in harmony with Oneness.

Chapter 19 — Beyond Duality

Our collective belief systems are indeed both a scaffolding that gives structure to our everyday consciousness and a tether that pulls us back whenever our consciousness might stray too far outside of the bounds of everyday reality. The scaffolding gives us a framework for perceiving and interpreting the world around us that enables our consciousness to stretch out and take in more, and the tether limits how far and wide our consciousness can go before we reach the limits. The whole human population holds and sustains such collective belief systems, and therefore, these systems are a key element in the story of humanity's spiritual evolution. They do indeed both lift and restrain humanity's potential for expanding the range of its consciousness.

Our long-term challenge is to evolve our collective belief systems so that they bring our lives into greater and greater harmony with Oneness. That guides the spiritual energy within all of us and opens new possibilities for humanity's evolution. We must indeed expand our spiritual horizon, but when our collective belief systems keep us from moving into greater harmony with Oneness, then we are all held back in our spiritual evolution. And like any scaffolding, there are some key structural pieces that hold our belief systems in place—some main pillars of the structure that need to be transformed if the whole structure is to change and evolve.

You see, some of our collective bubbles have a much more limiting effect than others. The bubbles with the most entrenched and often most subtle limiting effects are the ones that hold our collective consciousness in patterns of duality—often in direct contradiction of Oneness. What do I mean by 'duality' in this context? One explanation would be ways in which we limit our range of options into an 'either/or' choice—we are forced to choose between two options where one choice automatically excludes the other. Maybe this is an obvious point, but there is no 'either/or' in Oneness, because there is no separation between 'this' and 'that.' Such a choice keeps us stuck within limited belief systems, especially within beliefs that contradict Oneness. That is the simplest explanation.

Look sat the consequences. If someone asks you: "How are things going today?" Maybe you reply simply that things are either good or they are bad! One friend said something negative about another. Was it true or false? We routinely turn complex things into black or white, and then we rearrange the facts to justify the decision we have made. Once you believe that this is a good day or a bad day, you can interpret the whole rest of the day as either good or bad. Once you decide that your friend was right or wrong, the history of your personal relationship gets reinterpreted, and the significance of the 'facts' can radically shift.

Maybe a deeper explanation though is that a duality is a bubble that holds a limited, special reality in which the exclusion of one thing from another does indeed appear to be real. For example, it is indeed a bad day, or your friend is certainly a liar. When consciousness flows through a bubble of duality, it experiences the separation inside the bubble as a schism, and the schism causes a kind of leap in the continuity of consciousness. As our everyday culture fills up with more and more bubbles of duality, you can understand then how easily the flow of your everyday consciousness gets lost and misdirected, even when you are trying to live in a spiritual way. Your path becomes like a maze where the flow of your consciousness repeatedly leaps in the wrong direction. To tell you the truth, our collective reality is so interwoven with bubbles of duality that our consciousness can just seem stuck in a maze that it can't escape. That is how we can come to say 'Duality Consciousness,' because it all becomes a self-reinforcing system of separation and discontinuity that creates the impression that duality is a natural state of being and a normal part of our reality, while at the same time your spiritual path is full of inconsistences and contradictions.

And maybe before proceeding, it is useful to remind ourselves that the universe as it exists outside of us and outside of our limited bubbles doesn't have 'dualities.' For instance, what need does nature have for 'dualities'? Nature just is—no 'either/or' choices or exclusions from Oneness. No flower ever says to itself that it is the wrong color. "Pink, not blue?" We are the creators of this duality consciousness. We invented it, and we can change it. But it is not easy to step outside of the huge network of bubbles that maintain duality consciousness, because they are all around us and embedded in our everyday collective consciousness. We can hardly have a thought that doesn't suggest duality at some level. So, lets examine a few of the major pillars of duality consciousness in order to see them and understand them from the outside.

Emotional-Mental Duality

Our discussion of the light-body has already touched on this particular pillar of duality, one that is supported in our everyday collective consciousness. The emotional-mental duality has been with us for a very long time. It grew out of the largely western cultural notion of the mind-body dualism, and then it developed over the centuries to become deeper, broader, and more absolute. And this shows up in our popular culture as a competition between the rational mind and the emotions. This theme is especially prevalent in science fiction, because we are collectively exploring the dead-end into which this duality leads us. Believing in a separation between feeling and thought is one of the cornerstones of Duality Consciousness. We imagine that we can separate our emotions from our thoughts and our thoughts from our emotions. We imagine that these are two separate streams in our life, and holding onto the emotional-mental duality causes a schism in our flow of consciousness that we hardly ever question. The closer you look at the emotional-mental duality, the more it just evaporates in contradictions and impossibilities. For example, if you could really examine what is included in everybody's typical notions of emotion, you would know that it constantly overlaps into everybody's notions of thinking. Where does 'emotion' end and 'thinking' begin? Do you ever feel without also thinking?

If you have always thought that you experience the world separately in terms of emotion and thought, it is probably because you were brought up to think that way. But not all humans are part of this particular belief system. One way of stepping outside the bubble of the emotional-mental duality is to experience cultures with a different orientation, cultures in which emotion and thought are interwoven into a single flow. It is a very liberating perspective on life to move beyond the thinking of the western world as if its particular issues and conflicts characterized all of humanity. This kind of duality has a limited range, and as is often the case, the first step to breaking a bubble is to experience it from the outside.

In truth, all thought is intimately connected to feeling and *vice versa*, but we often act as if we are in denial about this. In part, that may be because much of our thinking evokes uncomfortable feelings. We just pretend that those feelings aren't there. For example, I have met so many people whose lives could be described as 'overly mental.' Many are mentally over-stressed and some are nearly burned out. If you ask to see their mental body, it is like an engine that is on the brink of breaking down or exploding. And along with this is often such a deep emotional blockage that it appears to be an absence of emotion. But look a little closer, and what you find is that, rather than being absent, emotion is quietly filled with pain and despair. The deeper reality is that this pain is part-and-parcel of this mental stress—that 'lack of emotion' is actually a product of denial and emotional shutdown. And the more emotions that are blocked, the stronger is the pattern of denial. We have just put on blinders to hide the negativity from ourselves.

But to be truly healthy and whole, you need to open yourself to feeling everything—open yourself up to experience the wide range of feelings that your thinking creates—feel with your thinking and think with your feeling. Your feelings reveal your truth when your thinking goes astray. You can visualize that the first step is bringing thought and feeling into a healthy balance. But ultimately finding a true unity of thought and feeling opens the way for further evolution. It is a doorway to knowing unity consciousness.

You can expand your capacity to experience emotion and thought as a unity if you learn to focus your attention in a different way. A good concept for capturing the true nature of this unity is the 'unity percept,' that is, to take in feeling and thought simultaneously in a blend—in particular, then to take in the world's events and happenings by blending their complexity of emotion and thought into a unity. Yes, an event may be examined in terms of emotions and thoughts, but that is typically a *post-hoc* observation. Events are the most natural way for a human being to organize their perception as a 'unity-percept.' It is essentially a kind of bubble that takes in the whole and binds diverse things together without separations. Consider an event of your life, and open yourself up to every aspect of it—take it all in as whole.

Unity-percepts have a sense of depth like works of art. They might contain an amalgam of diverse elements that are related together simply by virtue of being within scope of the percept. The qualities that you associate with the percept depend on you as a Creator Being. Every perception is the result of a creative act. And when we focus through unity-percepts, we engage our hearts and mind together—in unity. That is the core of being in Unity Consciousness, and it is something with which we need much more practice!

Male-Female Duality

It seems that our collective cultures can sustain bubbles of duality long after they serve any useful function. These bubbles may have once been advances in collective consciousness—yes, duality may have been a step along humanity's path of evolution—but duality bubbles have become an obstacle to expanding our consciousness in the era ahead. The emotional-mental duality is one of these. We tend to hold on to such collective bubbles and to prop them up until something significant happens to knock them over—that means until enough of society has been shaken up and broken out of the bubble.

Another collective duality bubble is the male-female duality. I don't mean the simple reality of male and female physiology; I mean what we have made of it and the baggage that we have attached to it. We seem to have conflated our physiology with restrictive social patterns of behavior and identity. At a certain stage of human development, the male-female duality may have appeared fundamental to everything in the world. It may have given a deeper significance and meaning to countless aspects of the world around us. Once upon a time, most people identified everything in the natural world as either masculine or feminine. And as human culture became more developed, this duality became increasingly formalized and elaborated, until it became more prescriptive and dogmatic. Today we have people living in modern cities who still carry the male-female programming patterns of earlier stages of human development.

Of course, our notions of gender have a biological origin, but our concepts around gender are exclusivity cultural. It is not that there aren't X and Y chromosomes—male and female. The problems arise when we try to fit human diversity into a duality-based concept of male-female—when we cross physiology with culture. Then the male-female duality becomes a culture-based limitation held in collective bubbles. Male excludes female, and female excludes male—it is a duality. And this issue of male-female duality is particularly prominent and vexing in our world today because we are collectively working through this issue.

I particularly wanted to discuss male-female duality in this book, because my perspective on it comes from the vantage point of being a healer and how it affects my clients. So many people have been entrained in the rigid stereotypes of masculinity and femininity—stereotypes that to some might seem inevitable and natural, but which are often sources of conflict and low self-esteem in others. Then too, many people have entangled male-female issues with those of victim and victimizer. One effect of this entanglement has been to hold people ever more deeply in the male-female schism, and at the same time it has obscured the more subtle aspects of the victimization that occurs in society. So much baggage!

Our collective goal needs to be stepping beyond such dualities as the male-female split. In modern society's myths and icons, the sacred feminine has been under-valued and the sacred masculine is almost entirely missing. A first step toward evolving a new concept of male-female is to recognize that we all have male and female aspects within ourselves. A second step is to establish a healthy balance between our male and female aspects. But balance isn't the final stage of evolution; balance still maintains a duality. Beyond balance is a unity in which male and female aspects are blended to form a continuity of possibilities. We need to perceive maleness and femaleness as aspects of a unity-percept that embraces the wholeness of many diverse qualities. There should be no separations. After all, most of our beloved spiritual guides and helping spirits are androgynous.

But right now, there are so many men who feel that they never live up to being the right kind of man, and women who feel that they never live up to being the right kind of woman. So many people are living in the shadow of never fulfilling what they were raised to believe they should be—they are trapped in the schism of feeling separated from something they should be. And there are so many relationships that fail because someone doesn't fit somebody else's model of the right male-female relationship. In truth, our full compass of male and female possibilities needs to be embraced.

One sign that I have seen of how fundamentally we are changing in regard to the male-female duality has arisen when working with the 'personality triangle.' This was originally taught to me by Amorah Quan Yin as one of the more subtle structures of the light-body. The original shape of the personality triangle captured the relationship of our male and female aspects to the self. It is a three-sided structure that holds a triangular shape. The personality triangle is also a reflection of the relationship of mother-to-father-to-child. But more recently in some sessions with my younger clients, the personality triangle has morphed into the personality circle. These clients did not seem to have categorical stereotypes of masculine and feminine. Their orientation was more fluid in a way that 'male' and 'female' roles had very flexible boundaries. Maleness-femaleness for them is a smooth continuum. There is nothing reflecting the departure from duality and the arrival in unity better than the circle.

Breaking the Bubble of Light and Dark

I want to share a story that has not always been easy for me to explain to others. I have deeply cross-examined myself on this, and I nevertheless feel certain about it. This experience was very important to my development as a healer. There was a time during my years of shamanic study when a dark entity came to stay in my light-body. I was a lot less experienced back then, and it took me a while to figure out just what had happened to me. I knew that something was there, but I went about my normal life just the same. The way that I recognized that this thing was a separate consciousness was by shifting my awareness into it and experiencing its reality. That was illuminating. I don't know why I didn't react to its being there with fear and why I didn't think to get rid of it immediately. I just seemed to know that it needed something from me, and maybe I could gain something from it. I was ok with that; I don't know why.

I spent time with the dark entity and watched the history of its life hunting and devouring things, especially destroying the rigidity that it disliked so much. It really hated churches and the hypocrisy it found there. It was working against what it considered the hypocrisy and arrogance of the light. It was dedicated to releasing what it perceived as stuck and out of alignment with Divine Creator's mandate to break free and grow! I learned to appreciate its nobility and its dedication to removing whatever was false in an attachment to the light. I began to understand its perspective. That led me to realize just how much the human customs and institutions of the light and of the dark can mirror one another. Broadly speaking both can be controlling and both can be liberating. I came to think that it is the removal of limitations that both the noble light and the noble dark work for, each from their own perspective, while at the same time there are ignoble elements of the light and the dark that impose restrictions and create stagnation. These are two essential aspects of human development, a bit like yin and yang. And both, what we normally think of as the realms of the light and the realms of the dark, include beings who are working against the free evolution of the human race. From this perspective, I came to believe that light vs. dark is not the genuine issue. There is a more subtle flow to how evolution is working itself out.

Back to my story, after some time, this dark entity just left. But I was changed. I had acquired a kind of tolerance and understanding of this dark being's perspective. I realized that the dark was not a monolithic force, and this had a practical impact on my life as a healer. I was able to visit some very dark places without judgment and meet the darkness within my clients without judgment. I have to conclude that my familiarization with this dark entity seems to have been part of my education. I have met other dark beings of the Earth who are important to the evolution of humanity and the Earth. I have also realized that many dark lords who I encountered were just as dedicated to the free evolution of All-That-Is as I was. They simply had a different mission.

I think too that my changed perspective on light and dark was reinforced by my encounters with the traditional Andean spiritual world. As far as I understand, traditional Andean cultures did not have a concept of light and dark or good and evil. Instead, I think that their perspective was anchored in the natural world and its processes. How do you explain beneficial vs. destructive events? They witnessed the Earth's overlapping processes of growth and decay as innate to Nature. The core challenge from their perspective was maintaining balance. The Andean lower world is full of beings who consume heavy energies. They have just as much right to exist as the beings of the upper world of refined spirits and the middle world of human beings. There is no battle of good and evil, but there is a constant search for balance in the giving and receiving among the three worlds. Balance in giving and receiving—that is central to Andean spirituality.

This idea of 'good' and 'evil' was a limited cultural invention, a creation of human beings, most specifically for us, an invention of Zoroastrianism in ancient Iran that became incorporated into our religions of Judaism, Christianity, and Islam. This idea didn't spread to all of the rest of the world, certainly not to the Americas—not until the age of European 'exploration.' Until the Europeans arrived, native peoples in the Americas had no idea that they had been excluded from the Garden of Eden.

And even within the contexts of the three traditional religions, any notion of balance between 'light' and 'dark' is not the final stage of evolution. Beyond 'light' and 'dark' is a unity, which is surrender to Divine flow, that is, accepting what happens without judgment and without the duality of good and bad. My best advice to any person trying to walk their spiritual path in today's polarizing world is to read every situation for exactly what it is. Everything that happens can be perceived as a unity-percept. Don't be drawn in to an opposition of 'light' vs. 'dark.' It is just another duality by which the ignoble light and the ignoble dark attempt to manipulate you. There is no opposition of light and dark. There is no separation. Once you have broken the bubble of light and dark, you will know.

Beyond Truth and Lies

Truth and lies are both bubbles. To understand this, lets first think about how a lie works. For some number of people, the lie is accepted as truth. The scope of what the lie is about is limited, and the number of people who accept it is limited. The lie is contained in a bubble that defines the boundaries of the lie. But sure enough, within that bubble the lie is the truth. And if you can view 'lies' in that way, then you might also come to see that a truth has a limited range and is accepted by a limited number of people—just like a lie. Every bubble of truth is accepted as absolute truth until it reaches and touches upon a greater truth, then that original bubble is revealed to be limited—not necessarily false, but limited in its scope of what it deals with. Newtonian physics defined absolute truth until relativity and quantum mechanics revealed it to be a limited truth. Maybe another way of looking at this would be to say that every bubble of truth is an approximation of a greater truth and that our bubbles of truth evolve as we discover better and broader approximations of the greatest truth, which is Oneness.

This relationship of truth and greater truth is exemplified in some of our everyday bubbles of truth that are actually quite limiting. These are often bubbles of collective truth that are either arbitrary or a poor approximation of a deeper truth. Our society often says that there is a right way of doing this and a wrong way of doing that. These prescriptions pose as truth, when in fact the greater truth is that they probably don't matter in any real sense at all. Then too, we can have personal bubbles of truth that may seem really important to us, but which have not kept up with our continuing process of growth and understanding. At one time we may have been convinced to hold onto every scrap of our money or else we would loose it. Later on, we learn the greater truth of generosity.

But the deeper learning comes with the realization that every situation involves multiple truths, some greater and some lessor. In that case, no one truth is absolute. Each truth comes with a perspective and is situated within a context. The perspective and the context shape the nature of the truth. This is so very clear when we consider relationships between people who have different perspectives on the same events. Each person's perspective and context is part of their own truth.

There is an evolution of our truth that usually comes in response to what underlying questions we asked. We usually start life with simple questions that are superseded by other questions. The newer questions change the scope of truth's boundaries. The simple pattern of believing in right-and-wrong with no shades of grey in between then becomes an act of denial—denial for shades of meaning or denial of the limited boundaries of truth. Denial is a bubble of untruth maintained in intentional opposition to a bubble of greater truth.

Maybe the limitedness of truth needs some examples. One of my clients experienced a very painful event with her family that caused her to be judged and cutoff from everyone. It was emotionally catastrophic for her because she thought that she had given so much to the family. The event was true and her pain and anger was real, and that is where she had gotten stuck, the initial stage at which things first occurred. After all, facts are facts. But the person's soul history cares only for the evolution of her soul-level knowledge, which is form of greater truth. Her healing process eventually resulted in a deeper understanding of how she had contributed to the situation, and that realization enabled her to release her pain and to create a more independent life for herself. The event was a teacher. The original facts were true, but her whole way of looking at it had been transformed. Her limited bubble of truth broke open into a bubble of greater truth and made her a better person.

I once had a friend, not a client, with an early life that included violence that haunted his adult years. The acts of violence were real, but after considerable personal work he came to understand how the violence was not just his alone, but he had been part of a collective system that for him included something like a strong tribal identification. It was only after taking in the bigger picture that he could fully separate himself from the context and completely own what he had done. He had long stopped blaming the people who were once the targets of his violence, and he began examining the whole system around the violence, including his friends, authorities, government, and the underlying social system. All had participated in creating his situation. And he was finding a road to peace. In all such cases, when the bubble of the original truth breaks open, the greater truth transforms one's sense of the meaning of that original 'truth' contained in the bubble. This is an example of the self-correction that happens when a bubble breaks. The facts of the original truth are reassembled in the context of the greater truth with wider boundaries. He found a way of forgiving himself.

The Law of One says that there is only one ultimate truth and that is Oneness. Every other truth is a limited truth. The boundaries around our truths expand as we move into greater and greater harmony with Oneness.

Toward Unity

Every one of the pillars of duality discussed here is a collective bubble that seems perfectly normal to most of the people most of the time. What happens when duality is released? Then there is the possibility of being in neutrality—of letting go of all the conflicting entanglements with their separations and schisms experienced through the bubbles of duality. When all of that is released, then you can find yourself in a new place. You have entered a different stage of human consciousness. The release of these core pillars of duality consciousness offers the opportunity to escape duality's pull of gravity. Instead, to release duality is to float—to float up and lift off because these separations are not holding you down. So don't fool yourself into thinking that being in neutrality is a mistake. Maybe you've been in the duality consciousness for so long that you might miss what you are used to. Arriving in neutrality can be a surprising experience. It can also be a huge moment of liberation—the moment that you are free of the bubbles that have kept your consciousness in a state of perplexity. Neutrality is a place of stillness and calm. Maybe you never experienced this really deeply before.

And you will want to stay in this place—to stay in neutrality even when walking in the everyday world, because it is not a place that you just visit. It is a state of being that emerges when you have released the bubbles that kept you in duality. And the more that you are able to release yourself from the constraints of duality bubbles, the deeper you can enter into this space. And here is a place to shine your inner light.

Part IV — Awakening

Chapter 20 — On the Path

"Does this path have a heart? If it does, the path is good; if it doesn't, it is of no use. Both paths lead nowhere; but one has a heart, the other doesn't. One makes for a joyful journey; as long as you follow it, you are one with it. The other will make you curse your life. One makes you strong; the other weakens you."
— Carlos Castaneda, *The Teachings of Don Juan: A Yaqui Way of Knowledge*

All paths may prepare you for awakening Oneness, but some paths are longer and more difficult than others. They lead you on a more difficult journey, a journey that you must ultimately complete within yourself while you try to escape from your maze of frustrating obstacles and illusions. These paths have been traveled a thousand, thousand times before, and that maze always leads you nowhere, as if maybe you had missed a hidden exit. Maybe there were lessons that the path was trying to teach you. You might ask yourself: "What have I missed over and over again?" Is it that as a Creator Being you actually have created the maze that you are struggling to escape? That you have created the limiting bubbles that hold you back? That you need to heal yourself in order to break free of your self-imposed limitations? Maybe you have been thinking that this isn't what happened to you. No you think: "Powerful forces overwhelmed me and left me with no other options." Cancel that idea. The power to leave the maze and to step forward on your path has always resided entirely within you. You are the only one who can break the bubbles and awaken Oneness in your life.

At this point, you certainly understand that your world, everything about how you perceive it, and everything that you think you know about it is held and sustained by bubbles. Your bubbles are the lens through which you perceive and understand everything outside of yourself—and even inside of yourself, because there is no inside and outside without bubbles that give your world its structure and meaning. And the bubbles are the direct manifestation of your innate ability as a Creator Being to create the meaning and the significance of the world around you. It is all your creation. And these bubbles are indeed a scaffolding that has in some ways lifted you up and in some other ways held you back. And therefore, it follows that you can determine the direction of your evolution by how you evolve your network of bubbles, and with that knowledge about yourself comes opportunities.

We have all arrived now at a new stage in our collective evolution, a stage that illuminates the landscape ahead of us in a new way, making visible the potential paths we have not yet chosen or not yet imagined. We come to the place of designing our path by our own conscious choice. How shall we do that? Can we do it in a way that "has a heart" as Castaneda describes?

In one sense, being on your path is about providing you with the preparation that you need for awakening Oneness within you. And in another sense, being on your path ultimately teaches you to release any sense of moving toward a destination that is out there ahead of you, maybe like every other spiritual goal you have known—because Oneness is not a destination. It is a state of being; it is what you are. And ultimately this state of being leads you into a mystery beyond your understanding. What could be a more exciting choice in life than to be on a mysterious path without a destination? Along the way you can take in the beauty that is all around you, and you can share your experiences with other seekers who are also on the path. And along the way there can be such freedom, because what defines this path is not a set of rules, but a continually evolving process of vision and choice. You imagine a world in alignment and harmony with Oneness, and then you give your energy to the bubbles that lead you to fulfill that vision. This is what happens when we manifest by conscious choice. Now, that is a path with a heart.

And there are so many others who themselves have discovered the possibilities of following conscious choice. They are each walking their path and contributing their personal vision of harmony with Oneness. Taken all together, we form a special collective bubble for creating and holding our collective vision. We have a collective desire to evolve and a collective power to create our world. And as we follow our path, we are giving energy to the bubbles that help us all to fulfill our shared vision.

As you personally stand at the threshold of the path before you, what do you know for sure? You know that you evolve, in fact, you know that all things are in a state of change. This is one of the few things that you really do know for sure. And if you observe the impact that you yourself have had on the world around you, you can begin to understand this in a very concrete sense. It seems to dawn on us only on rare occasions just how much we ourselves create the flow of energy moving all around us. There are so many examples of how you have changed your life in front of you right now in this moment if you will but simply observe them, not as predetermined outcomes that were beyond your influence, but as the dynamic result of the energy flow that you initiated. This teaches you that there has never been a fixed path ahead of you. Your path has always been something that you have created with each succeeding step. So without hesitations or reservations, you can now continue the process of moving your life into your next stage of evolution.

"But what do the guides want me to do?" That is a question that has often been asked by people contemplating the choices in their life. I think that the right answer to this question is to pose another question: "How do you think that the guides are supposed to answer if you haven't set your intentions for yourself?" We are the ones who must set our direction and then steer our course. After all, we are the Creator Beings.

And ironically, we have created a lot of ideas about master plans for humanity that are supposed to originate with someone other than ourselves. Have we perchance actually been trying to explain our complex past by telling ourselves that it was always somebody else's responsibility? This idea of having no control is an avoidance of the deeper truth that our path has always been our own choice and our own creation. But it would certainly help us on our path if we had a compass to steer by. And, of course, our guides do have a compass by which they navigate. It is the vision they hold of Oneness.

The Law Of One

As you proceed on your path, rather than searching for a master plan out there somewhere that gives you answers, maybe in a deeper sense 'the plan' is already built into you. If so, then it must be in harmony with Divine Creator's great dream experiment, and it must be deeply motivated by your desire to be in harmony with Oneness, because nothing else will resolve the tension of your core paradox of being finite and infinite— the two must become one. Your one sure guide, the needle of your compass so to speak, points to the Law of One: everything is the expression of one Light, one Source, one Divine Creator.

Anything that contradicts this, anything that suggests separations, is not the greater truth and must eventually fade away and disappear in your process of evolution.

"Ok, but how do I actually implement any of this in my life?" you might say. First, the Law Of One is a guiding principle that can transform your consciousness. Focusing on it shifts you ever closer to a consciousness of Oneness. Secondly, it gives you a measure by which you can steer your evolution toward Oneness. You may not always be able to envision exactly how you want to live, but you have this principle by which to guide your process of awakening. Every time that you feel the effect of separation in your life, every time that duality asserts itself, say: "This is not the greater truth, it is not my truth, and I hold that all is Oneness."

One could say too that the Law of One is the flip side of the bubbles. The bubbles are the temporary appearance of separateness that arises because you drift into a kind of creative dreaming in which you create separations. No thought or idea that is based on separation is a greater truth. It is only a brief moment's dream contained within a bubble. This is a reflection of how you are acting as an extension of Divine Creator. In this manifested dream that you call your life, your evolution is your own creative dream just like Divine Creator's great dream experiment!

Consider the greater meaning of the phrase "As it is above, so below." Its truest meaning is that there is no above and no below—no separation. There is only the One. You may think that you are just an individual person trying to hold a connection to the Cosmos and the Earth, but you are just as much the Cosmos and Earth holding a connection to you—no separation. The Law of One states that everything is Oneness. Another consequence of this is the recognition that everywhere you look, what you are seeing is the same as yourself, because you and the world are of one substance. Really take in the consequences of that. Light is simply seeing light. Oneness isn't 'out there.' The whole world reflects Oneness back to you if you will just recognize it.

And as you evolve, there are many other principles that you might think of as supporting the Law Of One. For example, all things strive to express their individuality and yet remain in harmony with Oneness. How can it be that the stuff of this world can possess this dual nature—to be part of Oneness and yet individuated in separateness? At first, it seems like a paradox. But once you recognize it and embrace it, you can also discover how to live and thrive in this paradox. You discover the joy of creating and expressing even the smallest everyday things in harmony with Oneness—especially creating and expressing feelings of love and wellbeing in harmony with Oneness. The Law of One is about resolving this most fundamental paradox—not as an insolvable question, but as the greater truth that finally shows us the way. You have the capacity and the opportunity to honor and love the unique individuality of all people, all things, all situations—to honor all individuality within All-That-Is while holding your connection to Oneness. This is exactly what Divine Creator's collective dream experiment is about.

The ultimate outcome of your work to heal yourself and to raise your consciousness is that the liberation of your consciousness itself brings healing, especially healing of your capacity to be your true self deeply and completely. Before it arrives, you have no idea how liberated your heart could be. Once you are there, your every path is a path with a heart.

Chapter 21 — A New Client, Part IV

It has been over a year since the last healing session with Ella that I wrote about. During that time she has completed the healing course with my wife, and she has become much more self-sufficient in healing herself. She radiates quite a different light today than she did when I first met her.

Ella has also explored relationships with a couple of men—looking for that healthy relationship that she wants for herself. She hasn't settled down and committed to any of these, but she is clearly more secure and confident in herself. That is easily observed in her body language.

After setting space, I ask her if she has some particular requests for this session, because she didn't email me any comments ahead of our session today.

E: "I was having a hard time putting anything into words. But I don't have a feeling about what next for me. Ok, I finished Ulla's course, and I experienced a lot of healing. I know that I feel lighter, and I am in better shape than I ever was before in my life, but I also have this feeling that something is missing. When I am at my job, I feel as if I am facing a different world. I mean just how is this supposed to work out? Where am I going?"

G: "Yeah, good questions, and you share some of the same questions with every person who has ever traveled down their spiritual path. Because there is a point, a point at which you discover that you are in a very different place from the people around you. Does that resonant with what you are experiencing?"

E: "Yes, yes. At work I kind of feel disconnected. Sometimes I feel as if I am totally in my own space. And I know that I am much more at peace with myself, and I am sure that shows. I think that there are a few people in the office who really respond to that aspect of me. But a . . . I don't know. Its confusing."

G: "I think that I know what you are describing. I can share with you how I think about it. Maybe that could be helpful for you. To me, you are in a state of transition that I recognize—a transition that is creating a shift in your outer-self. You have cleared away so many of the limitations and compulsions from earlier in your life that a lot of your old habits of mind and behavior aren't working anymore."

E: "Yeah, I think that I get that. And am clearing myself, and I am happy with the differences. Clearly, I don't get brought down by things so often. I don't get triggered or get so angry. But this is something different."

G: "Maybe you have heard the phrase: "In the world, but not of it."

E: "Yeah, that's it. I am living in two different worlds—back and forth—my spiritual life and work."

G: "I's say that it is one physical world, but two different ways of relating to it. I could say that there is an 'old self' and a 'new self,' or I could say a 'limited self' and a 'greater self.' Like many people before you, you have opened the doorway to your greater self."

I can sense that I am on point, because Ella looks a little shocked and she is breathing deeply. Her light-body's energy is shifting rapidly.

G: "Ahead for you are many possibilities—ways of becoming more whole. No one can tell you exactly how that will unfold for you personally. It is your path to walk, but others have walked similar paths before. There are some shared experiences, and there is companionship. Do you think that you are ready to move ahead?"

E: "More than anything. I want to be whole."

G: "One way that we can work together to take you through that doorway is to expand on your training. You have opened up your perception in the context of healing course. Your skills of perception can be extended into everyday life so that you 'read' the situations of your life just like you 'read' energy in healing. That is a way of extending that part of your self that has grown through your healings into every part of your life. In that way we bring the "two worlds" that you describe together. The 'you' who has grown in the 'Divine Oneness' course can grow and expand—to be more whole."

E: "Yeah, I go for that."

G: "Ok, we will continue with this in the next session, but for right now there is some healing work that I would like to suggest. This is what came up for me yesterday when I was planning for today."

E: "Sure enough."

G: "This is a healing process for helping you to come into greater wholeness. And once again, I would like us to work with your female and male aspects—this time with a different goal."

E: "What would you like me to do"

G; "First, I'd like to say that you have done a lot to clear away the programming that you originally carried. Your female and male aspects are much clearer and healthier than before."

E: "Yeah, I feel that too."

G: "I would like to go a step further and to help bring these aspects into greater wholeness, a unity in which they are more integrated. I'll guide you in the process, just sit back for now, close your eyes, and bring yourself back in touch with the work we did before on these aspects of yourself."

Ella sits back and moves into a trance-like state, like she has learned in her healing course.

G: "As you get back in touch with that work, how do you feel?"

E: "I feel ok. I am happy for all of the changes, but there is still some kind of tension."

G: "I want to focus on the male and female aspects from a higher frequency than before. I want you to focus on seeing your spiritual body. When you are ready, tell me what you see."

E: "It looks a little gray to me. And there is some kind of crack in it."

G: "Ok, so put your hands around your image and use your healing tools to clear it."

E: "I'll use full-palm a diamond laser light to clear it. And the crack?"

G: "Leave that for now. Let me know when the clearing is complete."

E: "Um-hmm."

G: "Now, I want you to ask to see the male and female aspect of your spiritual body. Let me know when you have that image in your mind."

E: "I have it. But one is mostly covering the other. It's the male side in front of the female side, and the female side is smaller than the male."

G: "Good. Put your hands around that image and give those two aspects whatever it is that they need to come into right relationship with one another."

While Ella is running energy on herself, I am also focusing on these two aspects of her spiritual body.

G: "Ella, how do they look now?"

E: "Better, I think. The female aspect has stepped forward more, but they don't look quite equal yet."

G: "I have a question for them: What holds the male and female aspects in separation?"

E: "Gosh, that goes to the heart. What is causing this imbalance anyway?"

G: "What I see is that the male aspect has taken on the role of feeling and has squeezed the female aspect out. Maybe it has taken over your spiritual guidance too."

E: "Yeah, this is pretty heavy."

G: "Lets both focus on the male aspect and give it what it needs to be at peace with the female aspect."

We both run energy for a few minutes.

E: "In my image, the male aspect has stepped to the side. I think that he didn't trust the female aspect and felt compelled to take over."

G: "I get that too. And I think that this distrust goes back to a prior lifetime in which you were a spiritual leader for a group of women. You made some errors of judgment that led to the group being attacked and killed. The people around you blamed this on your being a woman, and you took on the belief that it was your not being male that brought on this disaster."

E: "When was this?"

G: "Long ago. About 400 BC. Would you please cancel all contracts that you have with yourself to never let your female side take the lead in your life, especially not your spiritual life."

While Ella is cancelling these contracts, I am running energy on the bubble that contains this past life in order to break it.

G: "How do the two aspects look now?"

E: "They are standing side-by-side.

G: "Lets focus on the female aspect now."

E: "I don't get very much. She is still smaller than the male and rather closed up."

G: "What is the feeling underneath of that?"

E: "There is a lot of pain and sadness."

G: "Why don't you run energy to help release that? Let me know when you feel that things have shifted."

E: "She is standing tall now and seems bigger."

G: "To me there was a kind of implosion here that has probably been with you for many lifetimes. Importantly, the two aspects are much more balanced now. So, lets both focus on doing whatever is necessary to bring the male and female aspects together. We are back to the question of what holds them in separation."

We are both running energy, and something is changing. The two sides move closer and closer together. There begins to form a third aspect that is the merger of the other two.

G: "Let them merge together—however much they do naturally. We bring them into Oneness."

The two aspects continue merging as the energy separating them is dissolving away. Without something to hold them apart, they move to become one. I sense that there is something more.

G: "Ella, I sense that there is a resistance in the female side to really letting go and merging that is held mostly in the upper part of the torso. Can you relate to that?"

There is a pause during which Ella seems to be reflecting on something.

E: "What occurs to me is something I thought about recently. I think that I have a kind of a resistance to thinking like a woman. I have gotten used to thinking like a man, especially at work. Yeah, there needs to be a deeper level of feeling."

G: "That is beautifully said."

As we keep working, the blending of the two aspects continues. To me, there is a part in the middle that is blended and that has a character and quality that is different from either the male or female aspect. Something new is emerging.

After a while, I think that the blending is as complete as it can be right now.

G: "Ella, I think that this work is complete for today. How do you feel?"

E: "I don't know."

G: "Take a moment to bring yourself back and to open your eyes."

E: "Yeah, that was good—something different. I need to drink some water."

There is a glass of water right there for her. She is coming back into touch with herself.

To me, Ella's work over the last year has brought her energy field into greater and greater unity. Separations and anxieties that have been with her since her childhood are just not there anymore. To me she really is becoming her 'greater self.'

E: "Thank you. That was really good for me."

We close by thanking the guides and setting the date for the next session.

Chapter 22 — Birthing the True Self

Somewhere along your path of healing it happens. Maybe it is at a point when you have broken through just enough of your limiting bubbles that you discover yourself in a place of greater freedom. Freedom from what used to be your compulsions and your fears—freedom from having to deal with yourself and to look out for yourself all of the time. 'You' aren't the thing that matters any more. You are free of yourself. Your old self was always a kind of burden—a heavy sack that needed defending and protecting. Now you can't react that way any more. There is nothing to defend.

If you look out across the horizon that now lies before you, it is an open plain. There are so many possibilities ahead, and yet nothing is definite. It is a field of possibilities in which you can move in any direction. So, who *are* you now that you come to this new place? Once you cross over the threshold into this new world, in one sense there is very little choice. You have to be totally authentic; you have to be your true self. There is really no other workable option. No other way to be in harmony with this new environment that surrounds you—no other way to be in harmony with your inner Divine Light, with your Higher Self, and with Oneness. You have no choice other than to be true to yourself.

But the question of 'self'—who you are—takes on a new meaning. The self is something lighter, and there are new possibilities for the way in which your self can experience the world around you. There is freedom and openness. Your life is an open book, and the next pages in that book are blank. It is a bit like finding your note—that note that you can sing better than any other—the note that resonates throughout everything that you are as if it were the most natural thing in the world. You sing; that is what you do. And your song is the song of your true identity as a bridge between the Cosmos and Earth. Let it ring out! You are manifesting your true self.

Releasing the Old Self

The old self is a construct that you have carried around with you for a very long time. Yes, having a 'self' is a necessary thing, but carrying around your old self has become burdensome. Try this: let your old self answer the question: "Who am I?" Observe the answer—you might be surprised at just how tired and disempowered your old self has actually been.

Your old self is yet another collection of bubbles—bubbles you started creating early in life to explain your separation from others, then bubbles to define your identity, your place in the world, and on and on. And if you look closely, you recognize that these bubbles are propped up and supported by the bubbles of other people in your life. Psychically you've been often looking at yourself through other's eyes—maybe through the eyes of your parents or siblings or co-workers. The bubbles that other people hold onto about you, these become the most powerful influence in maintaining your old self. And therefore, it is important to realize how much those bubbles are really about them. It is time for you to withdraw your energy from their bubbles. You can say to yourself, "This is nothing about me!" When you realize that others don't really see you, that they are only projecting parts of themselves on to you, then you are outside of the bubble of the old self that they support. You are ready for the true self.

Guardian of the Open Plain

It often happens near the end of releasing the old self that some challenge emerges from deep within you. It is something in you that resists the release of the old self and which creates a roadblock on your path of progress. In my experience, it is often something built into your personality during your first three years of life—something so fundamental that you hardly know how to put a name on it. This final barrier is often connected to your core anxiety that you may now experience in the way that you experienced it as a small child. This is no easy task. It is a final reckoning—a final step of facing up to your deepest fears. It is like a guardian that stands before the open plain trying to block you from entering the realm of the true self.

And how do you get past this guardian? I think about the final initiations that spiritual aspirants in ancient Egypt used to face in the great pyramid. A major challenge for the initiates was to be sealed in the stone sarcophagus where they faced their fear of death. But I think that death wasn't the only issue. The other issue was life. How do you face your primal fear of living?

My experience is that when you face that open plain before your true self, then one way or another you must make peace with whatever comes forth to hold you back. You must feel it, acknowledge it, and let it move on in exactly the same way that you have faced and healed every other dilemma of your life. While on the path of healing, you have practiced this transition so many times that it becomes like a dance step that you can execute without thinking. Somehow—by instinct or conscious effort— you find your way to neutrality. Then, as you move past the guardian and begin to enter into that open plain as the true self, everything will seem to have changed. And you are truly free like pure energy, like the wind blowing across the plain.

Evolving A New Collective Consciousness

Humanity is evolving, and today's evolution is leading to a new shared state of consciousness. It is a new collective consciousness sustained by a network of bubbles that are home in the reality of the open plain. It is a 'state of consciousness' because these bubbles give the flow of consciousness a new framework for stability. Call it unity consciousness, or Christ consciousness, or fifth-dimensional consciousness—it is a state of consciousness in which everything is connected. It emerges naturally when you have released your old self. When you truly let go of the separations, you find that it has been waiting for you all along.

> "We ask at this time for a field of divine Unity Consciousness. A field of divine Unity Consciousness to help us step out of all duality thinking and perception, to help us see and experience the unity in all things."

Unity consciousness is its own reward. Just experiencing that shift in yourself is enough. You feel more complete. You feel more whole. Unity consciousness does not need to be a kind of achievement like ascension or enlightenment. It doesn't need to be related to acquiring spiritual power, or being safe, or being happier or healthier. These are all fine things, but the extent of these things in your life is not a measure of the state of your consciousness. They are not requirements for higher consciousness, nor can you gain this kind of consciousness by possessing them. Consciousness is a domain of its own. It does not need to serve any other purpose in your life other that this: you are in Unity Consciousness and that is itself the reward.

Unity Consciousness is not a state that you experience only in meditation or other special occasions. It is a change in you that you will carry with you into everything that you do. When you reach the stage of carrying Unity Consciousness into in the everyday world, you will draw upon your creative capacities to recalibrate your everyday world in alignment with Unity. You re-create your world, and you join others in creating this new reality of Unity.

And yet Oneness Consciousness is something beyond the open plain. What Oneness Consciousness is for all of us is visible on the distant horizon. It is a place that we can meet after we have learned how to cross the open plain.

> *"We ask that the seed of Divine Oneness be planted within us so that our lives blossom in ever greater harmony with Oneness."*

We are a bit like young plants whose leaves are reaching for the sun. We can't touch the sun, but we can sense its direction. And as we reach higher and higher, our branches and leaves take on a unique character and structure that is shaped by our quest. Our foliage becomes an expression of our reaching toward the sun. Harmony with Oneness is a process of growth. Each new step that you take as your true self creates a connection to Oneness that never existed before. There is nothing to measure, nothing closer or farther, until we create it. And when we create it, then it stands in a relationship to the Oneness that can only be sensed within yourself. And as you move forward step by step in this process, your true self and the whole of what you are comes more and more into harmony with Oneness, like you are reaching for the sun.

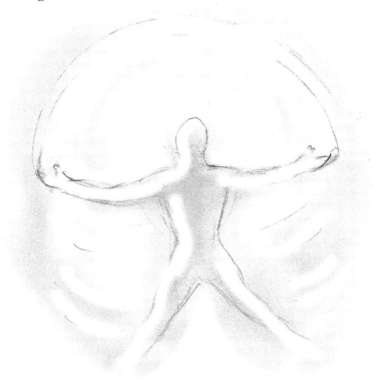

What is it like to awaken one day to Oneness? It changes everything from the inside out. Awakening to Oneness breaks through your limitations and conventional thinking. In the experience of Oneness old preconceptions fall apart, and urgency is eroded, fear becomes unnecessary, and grief is a temporary illusion. There is the joy of Divine Light that shines out from within you. There is the presence of Divine Creator in everything around you. And in this place, your connection to the Earth becomes a celebration, because there are no separations. The Earth is you, and you are the Earth. All humanity is you and you are all humanity. It is in the light of this experience that you must ultimately create your way of making sense of Oneness. You will do this as a part of your intrinsic nature.

"Go break some more bubbles," Divine Creator says. *"You'll figure out the rest."*

Of course, you are breaking bubbles and making the bubbles of a new collective consciousness. It is your creativity as a Creator Being that empowers you to brake and remake the bridge of bubbles that fills the space between the finite and the infinite even while you are walking your path in the physical world. You long to be in Oneness at all times and in all places. All of your creations are an act of love that is seeking fulfillment. It is to live among the many possibilities of All-That-Is and still to manifest from the Divine Light within yourself. That is the truth of Divine Creator's dream. You hold the Divine Light within yourself, and yet here you are on Earth. You are a finite being and part of the Oneness. Now is truly to live it.

MEDITATION: Oneness of Cosmos and Earth

We are the bridge between the Cosmos and the Earth, and this is a fundamental aspect of our being. In this meditation you connect yourself to both the Cosmos and the Earth in order to bring them with yourself into Oneness.

1. Close your eyes, ask for a field of Divine Oneness, ask for the presence of your guides, and balance your auric field just as you did for the first Meditation: I Am Oneness.
2. Focus all of your attention on the Earth as a conscious being.
3. Observe it as a realm of light—as perceiver and perceived.
4. Move deeper, blending with the Earth, and becoming one with it. Say to yourself: "I am the Earth," and hold that state as long as you like.
5. From within your connection to the Earth, focus all of your attention on the Cosmos as a conscious being.
6. Observe it as a realm of light—as perceiver and perceived.
7. Move deeper, blending with the Cosmos, and becoming one with it. Say to yourself: "I am the Cosmos," and hold that state as long as you like.
8. Ask that you, the Earth, and the Cosmos be merged in Oneness. Absorb yourself in the state of consciousness that this creates. Let this move through everything that you are. Hold it for as long as you like.
9. When you are ready, simply open you eyes and stay sensitive to what the meditation has opened up.

Postlude — A Meeting of Strangers

What a strange outcome you might say, "One result of my healing process is an odd feeling of being alone. I am in this new place with myself where I feel more whole and complete in myself than ever before. I feel lighter and clearer, but this has also changed my relationship to everything and everybody around me."

In a very important sense you do become the stranger. You may find that the people around you are concerned and preoccupied with things that you can't identify with. You can't connect to their sense of urgency. You just can't imagine getting involved in their dramas. Maybe you used to enjoy such things—you just loved people's ups and downs with their bits of this and that—but now you can't even fake it. It is not possible to think of taking on another person's burdens or their anxieties. It was hard enough healing yourself and liberating your own Divine Light. You don't take on such things any more. You focus now on what is *your* truth and you strive to be in the very best harmony with Oneness that you can. And this feeling of detachment isn't because you lack empathy for others. You have lots of empathy—deep love and acceptance for other people and for the challenges they are facing. It isn't about lack of feeling—there is just a different kind of feeling. In fact, you have a deep feeling for the whole of life and the Earth. If you just open yourself up, you can feel everything.

Where have you arrived then? What is this world where you

have always lived and yet which is strangely unfamiliar? This shift can feel a bit like moving through a tunnel, because there is a transition in which the old way of being in the world slowly disappears from view before the new way of being fully reveals itself to you. At the end of the tunnel you arrive in what seems like a different world. And moving through the tunnel, you cannot take your old 'ways of being' with you, no matter how much you think that you can't survive without them. The situation is a bit like being at the airport with your luggage stuck in the X-ray machine. Guess what? It isn't coming with you. Let it go and move on with your journey. Only the 'you' who is totally free of your baggage will get through that tunnel.

And at the same time, here you are still standing in the everyday world where you can observe the qualities of life going on around you. I say 'observe' because you know in your heart that you are just not 'in the world' like you used to be. Maybe you can't believe other's beliefs. Certainly you can't join those cycles of victimhood or support those patterns of denial. Maybe it seems obvious to you that people are in their own bubbles reacting to their own creations. Maybe your old keys just didn't fit those locks anymore.

And the feeling is particularly acute for the people who have been closest to you—your old friends, your family, and your children. You are both so close to them—you know them so well—and somehow there is a distance. You have come to a place of loving neutrality—we might even say 'extra-sensitive' neutrality, because this is not about cutting off anything around you. It is about your standing in the open plain by yourself.

Maybe the biggest unexpected challenge here is the shift in your source of energy. In your ordinary relationships you have given and received energy from others. I am not talking about co-dependency or the ways that we give up our power. I am talking about the ordinary exchanges of energy that are part of our families and close friends. We take in energy from others, but once we go through the tunnel and enter the open plain, then you cease to take energy from others or to give energy away. You experience the ultimate responsibility for yourself—to walk in the world without taking from others and without giving away to others what is not theirs—to be invisible at the level of the ordinary world's energy—to walk without leaving footprints. That is why on the open plain we have the freedom to move anywhere—just like the wind.

At the same time that this shift happens, another source of energy opens up to you. We can call it the great Cosmic well. Deep in the heart of the Cosmos is a place that holds a connection to you, and it is from that place that you draw the energy that supplants what you once took from others. You become self-sustaining. This is the deep mystery to becoming a stranger to the old world—you become intimate with the heart of the Cosmos.

Deep within yourself, you know that you wanted this and why you find yourself in this place now. You wanted to move on into the next stage of evolution as a human being. You wanted to enter into the greater reality that has been waiting there for you. Whether you consciously knew it or not, you wanted to move through the tunnel into this other world. You knew it was there, even if you couldn't totally anticipate what it would be like for you.

And how have things changed so totally? You understand that the world you once knew was a product of bubbles that created the significance and the meaning of what you experienced. Those bubbles held your everyday reality and your belief systems, as well as your understanding of your 'self.' These bubbles were invisible, and yet they determined how everything was perceived and understood. As you look about you now, clearly your physical world is the same as it was before, but the significance of everything that you feel is totally transformed. Maybe that is why you feel differently about the physical world—so much more at peace.

There is a sense of the profound even in the minutia of everyday life. That is what liberation feels like. It is the liberation to experience the deep spiritual significance of life. The reality of your old world has been rewritten, rewired, and gotten plugged into something different—plugged into the bubble of a different reality. You share the same physical reality with everyone else, but the reality you experience is very different. Welcome to the New Earth!

That is how you become a stranger. You become a stranger to your old world, but you are an explorer in a new world. It is a beautiful journey how you have followed the path of healing and passed through the tunnel to discover a new way of being on the open plain. And then what? What do you do next? You don't need a plan. You are the manifestation of the plan to be in this new world—in fact, to help create this new world. By making your way to this place, you are already helping to manifest this new world for all of humanity. When you experience these changes, you become an influence on everyone around you. Your change is broadcast on all of the psychic channels. You help to shift the collective toward a new consciousness. And when enough people experience these changes, then the total collective can never be the same again. The collective bubbles that sustain and restrain humanity will be broken and recreated anew. It will be a new era in human consciousness.

To be a fully empowered human being walking the Earth in

grace and beauty is all that you have to be. As Divine Creator has said, "You'll figure out the rest." You can't help yourself. You are a Creator Being. Work to put your feet fully down in this new world and to fulfill the task for which you were created—to be the bridge between the Cosmos and the Earth. This is a place from which you are meant to create something new. You arrive as a pioneer in the place to which humanity is evolving—the New Earth. It is nothing less than the collective bubble of New Earth consciousness, a new culture for humanity—a culture that can guide humanity's evolution into greater and greater harmony with Oneness that is your guiding light.

A Meeting Of Strangers in the New Earth

And of course, even as strangers, we seek the companionship of others who are like us making this transition to living on the other side of the tunnel—others walking the Earth like us in the psychic space of the open plain. We are not alone on this journey.

Lets make a plan. The plan is to meet one another on the other side of the tunnel—to arrive in the New Earth, and to recognize each other there. It is a bit like sailing to the 'new world' in the hope of joining others there like yourself to make a new life. Yes, we will meet this time in the New Earth and know each other—to recognize ourselves as companions in awakening Oneness.